Contents

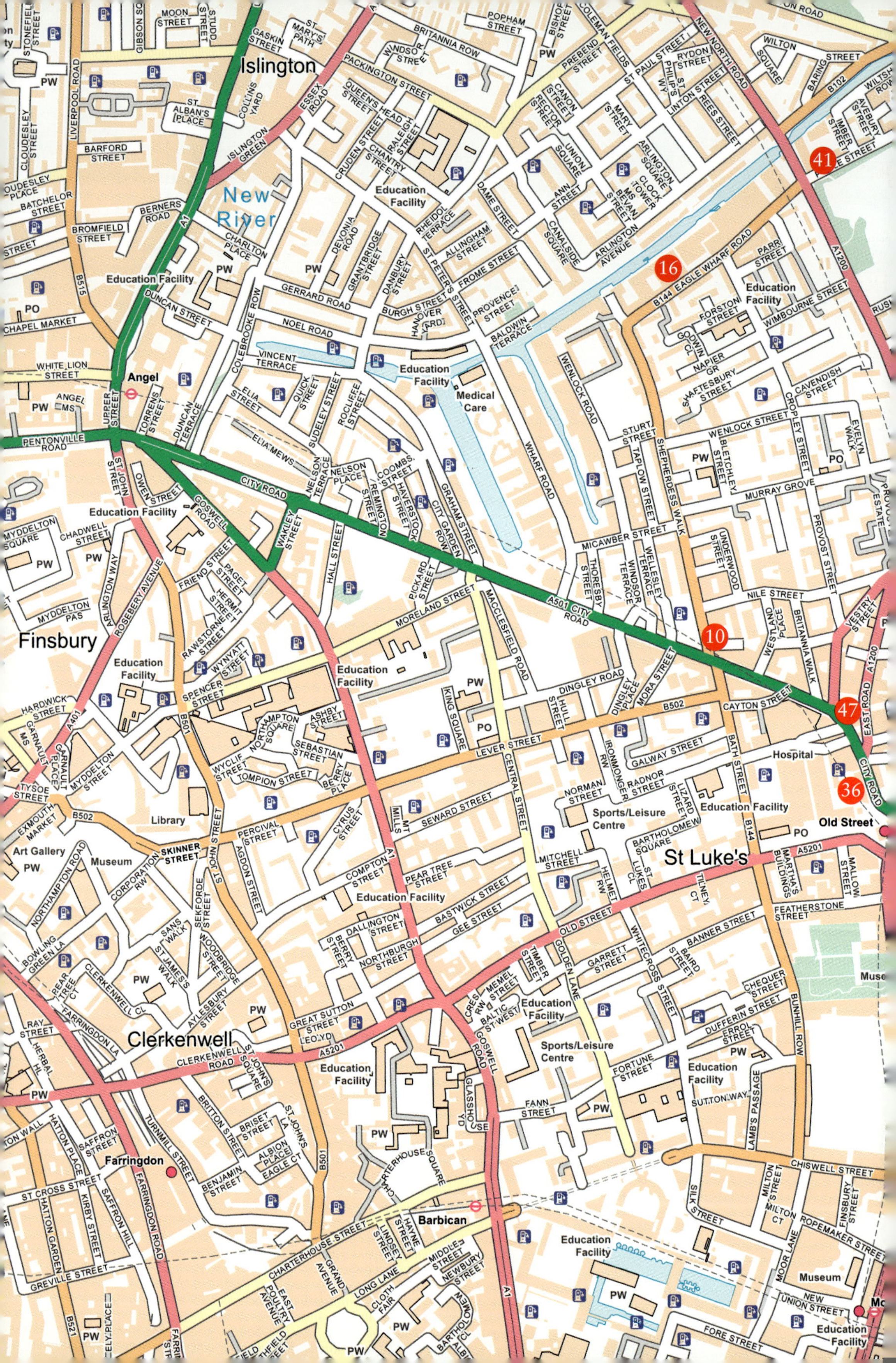
Islington
New River
Angel
Finsbury
Clerkenwell
St Luke's
Farringdon
Barbican
Old Street
City Road
Pentonville Road
Goswell Road
Old Street
Clerkenwell Road
Education Facility
Medical Care
Hospital
Sports/Leisure Centre
Museum
Library
Art Gallery
16
41
10
47
36

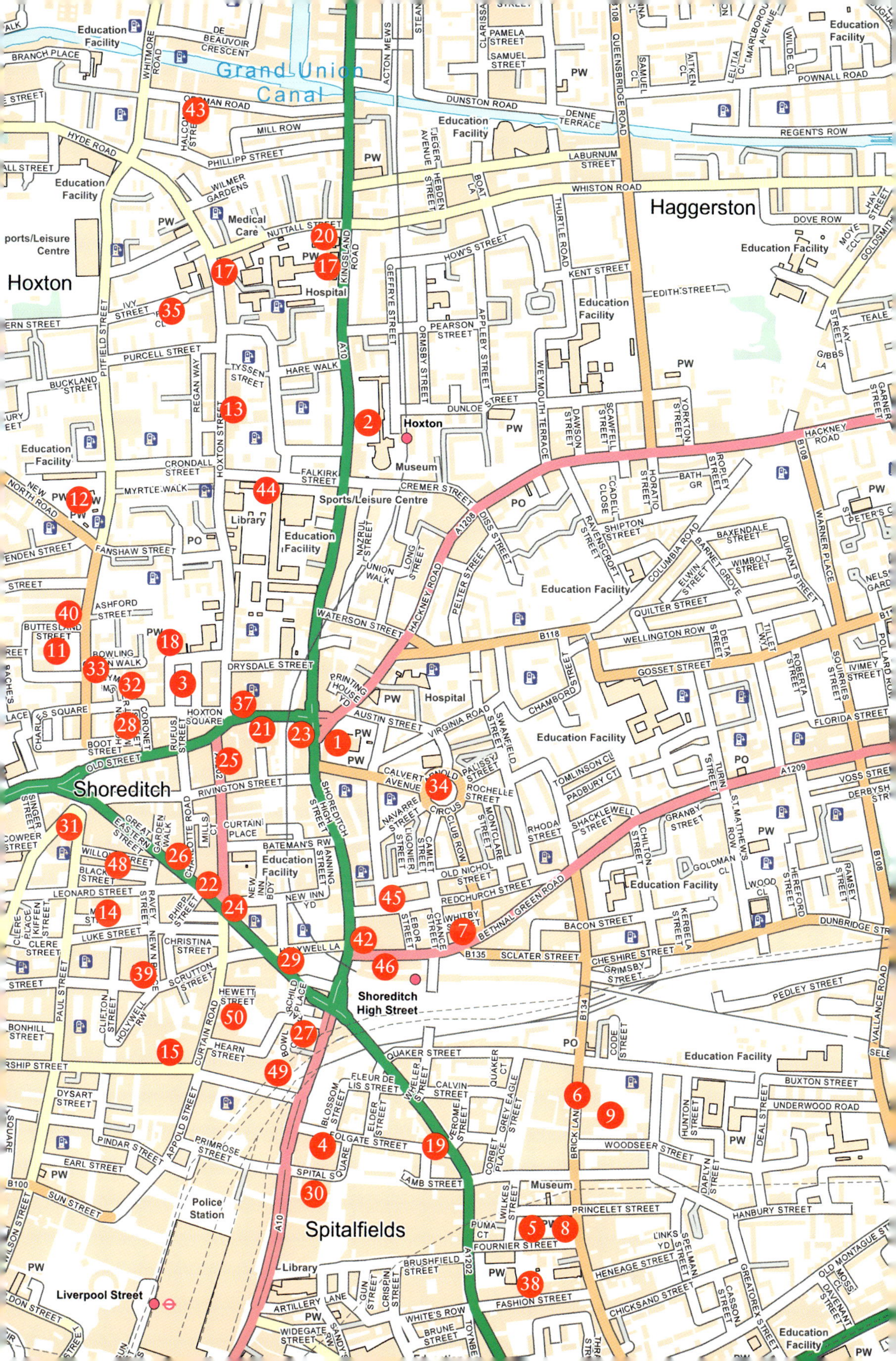
Grand Union Canal
Hoxton
Haggerston
Shoreditch
Spitalfields
Education Facility
Sports/Leisure Centre
Medical Care
Hospital
Hoxton
Museum
Library
Police Station
Liverpool Street
Shoreditch High Street
PW
PO
DE BEAUVOIR CRESCENT
BRANCH PLACE
WHITMORE ROAD
ORSMAN ROAD
MILL ROW
HYDE ROAD
PHILLIPP STREET
WILMER GARDENS
NUTTALL STREET
KINGSLAND ROAD
IVY STREET
PITFIELD STREET
PURCELL STREET
BUCKLAND STREET
TYSSEN STREET
HARE WALK
REGAN WAY
HOXTON STREET
CRONDALL STREET
MYRTLE WALK
FALKIRK STREET
NEW NORTH ROAD
FANSHAW STREET
ASHFORD STREET
BUTTESLAND STREET
BOWLING GREEN WALK
DRYSDALE STREET
HOXTON SQUARE
CHARLES SQUARE
CORONET STREET
BOOT STREET
OLD STREET
RUFUS STREET
RIVINGTON STREET
CURTAIN PLACE
BATEMAN'S ROW
NEW INN YARD
GREAT EASTERN STREET
GARDEN WALK
CHARLOTTE ROAD
MILLS COURT
SINGER STREET
COWPER STREET
WILLOW STREET
BLACKALL STREET
LEONARD STREET
CLERE PLACE
KIFFEN STREET
CLERE STREET
LUKE STREET
RAVEY STREET
PHIPP STREET
CHRISTINA STREET
SCRUTTON STREET
HOLYWELL LANE
HOLYWELL ROW
CLIFTON STREET
PAUL STREET
BONHILL STREET
HEWETT STREET
CURTAIN ROAD
HEARN STREET
BOWL COURT
PLUMBERS ROW
WORSHIP STREET
DYSART STREET
APPOLD STREET
PINDAR STREET
PRIMROSE STREET
EARL STREET
SUN STREET
WILSON STREET
SHOREDITCH HIGH STREET
A10
A1202
QUAKER STREET
FLEUR DE LIS STREET
BLOSSOM STREET
ELDER STREET
FOLGATE STREET
SPITAL SQUARE
WHEELER STREET
CALVIN STREET
VEROME STREET
LAMB STREET
CORBET PLACE
GREY EAGLE STREET
WILKES STREET
PUMA COURT
FOURNIER STREET
PRINCELET STREET
BRUSHFIELD STREET
GUN STREET
CRISPIN STREET
ARTILLERY LANE
WHITE'S ROW
BRUNE STREET
WIDEGATE STREET
SANDY'S ROW
FASHION STREET
TOYNBEE STREET
ACTON MEWS
DUNSTON ROAD
CLARISSA STREET
PAMELA STREET
SAMUEL STREET
HEBDEN STREET
YEGER AVENUE
BOAT LANE
LABURNUM STREET
WHISTON ROAD
THURTLE ROAD
QUEENSBRIDGE ROAD
B108
DENNE TERRACE
REGENT'S ROW
POWNALL ROAD
DOVE ROW
KENT STREET
EDITH STREET
HOW'S STREET
GEFFRYE STREET
PEARSON STREET
ORMSBY STREET
APPLEBY STREET
WEYMOUTH TERRACE
DUNLOE STREET
DAWSON STREET
SCAWFELL STREET
HORATIO STREET
YORKTON STREET
HACKNEY ROAD
CREMER STREET
A1208
DISS STREET
NAZRUL STREET
UNION WALK
LONG STREET
PELTER STREET
RAVENSCROFT STREET
CADELL CLOSE
SHIPTON STREET
COLUMBIA ROAD
BARNET GROVE
ELWIN STREET
BAXENDALE STREET
WIMBOLT STREET
DURANT STREET
WARNER PLACE
QUILTER STREET
WATERSON STREET
B118
WELLINGTON ROW
DELTA STREET
TILLET WAY
GOSSET STREET
ROBERTA STREET
SQUIRRIES STREET
IVIMEY STREET
PRINTING HOUSE YARD
AUSTIN STREET
VIRGINIA ROAD
CHAMBORD STREET
SWANFIELD STREET
FLORIDA STREET
CALVERT AVENUE
ARNOLD CIRCUS
PALISSY STREET
ROCHELLE STREET
TOMLINSON CLOSE
PADBURY COURT
TURIN STREET
A1209
VOSS STREET
DERBYSHIRE STREET
NAVARRE STREET
LIGONIER STREET
CAMLET STREET
CLUB ROW
MONTCLARE STREET
RHODA STREET
SHACKLEWELL STREET
CHILTON STREET
GRANBY STREET
ST MATTHEW'S ROW
GOLDMAN CLOSE
WOOD CLOSE
HEREFORD STREET
RAMSEY STREET
OLD NICHOL STREET
REDCHURCH STREET
BETHNAL GREEN ROAD
EBOR STREET
CHANCE STREET
WHITBY STREET
BACON STREET
KERBELA STREET
DUNBRIDGE STREET
B135
SCLATER STREET
CHESHIRE STREET
GRIMSBY STREET
PEDLEY STREET
VALLANCE ROAD
B134
CODE STREET
BRICK LANE
BUXTON STREET
UNDERWOOD ROAD
HUNTON STREET
DEAL STREET
WOODSEER STREET
DAPLYN STREET
HANBURY STREET
LINKS YARD
SPELMAN STREET
HENEAGE STREET
CHICKSAND STREET
CASSON STREET
GREATOREX STREET
OLD MONTAGUE STREET
DAVENANT STREET
B100

Key

1. Church of St Leonard, No. 119 Shoreditch High Street, E1
2. Museum of the Home, No. 136 Kingsland Road, E2
3. Hoxton Square, N1
4. Dennis Severs' House, No. 18 Folgate Street, E1
5. Fournier Street – Gilbert & George, E1
6. Brick Lane and Beigel Bake, E1
7. Nos 3 and 5 Club Row, E1
8. Jamme Masjid Mosque, No. 59 Brick Lane, E1
9. The Old Truman Brewery, Brick Lane, E1
10. Eagle Tavern & Former Grecian Theatre, No. 2 Shepherdess Walk, N1
11. Former Aske's Almhouses and London College of Furniture, Pitfield Street, N1
12. Church of St John the Baptist, Pitfield Street, N1
13. Hoxton Hall, No. 130 Hoxton Street, N1
14. Former Church of St Michael and All Angels, Mark Street, EC2
15. Nos 91–101 Worship Street, EC2
16. Nos 49–50 Eagle Wharf Road, N1 (now, Holborn Studios)
17. Relief Office, St Leonard's Hospital, Hoxton Street and Kingsland Road, N1
18. Church of St Monica, and the Priory of the Augustinian Friars, Hoxton Square, N1
19. Former Peabody Housing, Nos 135–153 Commercial Street, E1
20. Former Church of St Columba, Kingsland Road, E2 (now Christ Apostolic Church)
21. Shoreditch Town Hall, No. 380 Old Street, EC1
22. Nos 40–42 Great Eastern Street, EC2
23. Wells & Co. Commercial Ironworks, Nos 125–130 Shoreditch High Street, E1
24. The Old Blue Last and The Theatre Playhouse, No. 38 Great Eastern Street, EC2
25. Nos 134–146 Curtain Road, EC2
26. Nos 43–49 Charlotte Road and Gloria Restaurant, EC2
27. The Crown and Shuttle Public House, No. 226 Shoreditch High Street, E1
28. Hoxton Market Christian Mission, Coronet Street, N1
29. Village Underground, No. 54 Holywell Lane, Shoreditch, EC2
30. Galvin la Chapelle, No. 35 Spital Square, E1
31. The Old Fire Station, No. 140 Tabernacle Street, EC2
32. National Centre for Circus Arts, Coronet Street, N1
33. Former Passmore Edwards Free Library and Courtyard Theatre, Pitfield Street, N1
34. The Boundary Estate and Arnold Circus, E2
35. No. 54 Ivy Street, The Ivy Street Family Centre, N1
36. Imperial Hall, former Leysian Mission, Nos 104–122 City Road, EC1
37. The Courthouse Hotel, Shoreditch. Former Magistrates' Court and Police Station, Nos 335–337 Old Street, EC1
38. Fashion Street Arcade, Nos 10–48 Fashion Street, E1
39. Zetland House, Nos 5–25 Scrutton Street, EC2
40. No. 55 Pitfield Street, N1
41. Gainsborough Studios, Poole Street, N1
42. The Tea Building, No. 56 Shoreditch High Street, E1
43. The Stag's Head Public House, No. 55 Orsman Road, N1
44. New City College, Falkirk Street, N1
45. Boundary Shoreditch, Nos 2–4 Boundary Street, E2
46. Boxpark, Nos 2–10 Bethnal Green Road, E1
47. City Road – Contemporary Architecture, EC1
48. Nobu Hotel Shoreditch, Nos 10–50 Willow Street, EC2
49. Principal Place and Principal Tower, Worship Street, EC2
50. The Stage, EC2

Introduction

Gritty, edgy, vibrant, cool – all have been used to describe the areas we know as Shoreditch and Hoxton today, but this was not always so. Lying just east of the City of London, these districts like Clerkenwell and Southwark were considered unorthodox and their entertainments including playhouses, inns, taverns and animal baiting were frowned upon and outlawed by the City authorities.

Shoreditch and Hoxton have a history as religious centres and were home to both the Holywell Priory, located around today's Curtain Road, and St Mary Spital, just behind Bishopsgate alongside Spitalfields Market. These two priories were founded in the late twelfth century as Augustinian monasteries. The latter had its own infirmary, one of the largest in medieval England, and was formally known as the Priory and Hospital of St Mary Spital. Both were sizeable institutions and served their local communities well until they were forced to close in 1539 under the Dissolution of the Monasteries and their lands and buildings were subsequently either demolished or sold to new owners. Although none of the original buildings remain standing, recent archaeological excavations have been conducted on their sites and have resulted in the exciting discoveries of part of a late sixteenth-century theatre at Holywell Priory and mass burial pits containing more than 10,000 bodies at St Mary Spital.

It is practically impossible to place a boundary on Shoreditch and Hoxton for it is continually evolving and each person one talks to seems to have a different take on the extent of its reach. Even more confusing is the fact that although primarily sitting within the London Borough of Hackney, the areas spill over to the neighbouring boroughs of the City of London, Islington and Tower Hamlets. So for the purposes of this book I have placed them within a zone that stretches between the Regent's Canal in the north, Brick Lane in the east, Spitalfields in the south and Old Street in the west. In terms of buildings that have been selected (far from an easy task!) I have tried to keep within these limits but may from time to time have slipped into neighbouring areas such as Spitalfields, for which I apologise.

The origin of the name Shoreditch is much disputed; popular myths assert that it is derived from Jane Shore, mistress of King Edward IV, who died and was buried in a ditch hereabouts, but it is equally plausible that it comes from 'soersditch' – recording a drain or sewer that once existed here. A third possibility is that it is named after the Soerdich family, who were lords of the manor in the 1300s. Whatever its origins, Shoreditch is very much associated with the creative and tech industries and is nowadays bursting with energy; many of its workers are tech entrepreneurs innovating technology and engaged in new and emerging businesses whether it be in the finance, media, fashion, music, food or property industries. Much of the area's crumbling commercial buildings have been gentrified and many new developments, both office and residential, have been and continue to be constructed. Large tech firms such as Amazon have chosen to locate their UK headquarters here and the streets around Old Street and the so-called Silicon Roundabout are filled with tech, media and film production businesses including such names as Adobe and Inmarsat, giving rise to the name 'Tech City'.

While Hoxton was originally a tiny hamlet on the boundary of the City of London, Shoreditch was an established parish for centuries and has been in existence from the time the Romans built Ermine Street almost 2,000 years ago. The busy major road still passes in front of St Leonard's Church (now mainly referred to as Shoreditch church) and Shoreditch High Street and Kingsland Road continue to follow its line. By the mid-eighteenth century Hoxton was partially built up but its main growth took place from the 1800s when its fields and pastureland disappeared and were replaced by housing, factories, yards and small workshops, as well as stables and market gardens.

Shoreditch in contrast had been a major force of the literary and entertainment scene since the Elizabethan era. It was in its streets that two of London's earliest theatres, the Theatre and the Curtain, were based, and both were enormously popular with Londoners unable to access such activities within the confines of the City of London. Run by the Burbage brothers, these were where William Shakespeare's plays were staged and where he himself performed. It is believed that several of his plays were premiered at the theatres, as well as those of Ben Jonson and Christopher Marlowe. So many of the actors lived close to the theatres and were parishioners of St Leonard's Church, Shoreditch, that it became known as the 'actor's church'. The theatres ultimately closed but entertainment remained very much an integral part of the district; throughout the seventeenth and eighteenth centuries it was filled with archery ranges, pleasure gardens, pubs and taverns and then in the 1800s music halls became all the rage, entertaining thousands of working-class men and women in their grand halls around Shoreditch, including Shoreditch Town Hall and Hoxton Hall. Although the music halls died out long ago, both these venues continue to provide the local community with stimulating theatrical, performance and musical programmes, as well as offering a fabulous range of events that include workshops, gigs, talks and film screenings. They represent the very spirit of present-day Shoreditch and Hoxton, which, since the late twentieth century, has been home to contemporary artists such as Damien Hirst, Tracey Emin, Gilbert and George and the street artists Banksy and Roa. Not only are art galleries in abundance here but practically every building contains an exterior wall or two covered in amazing colourful street art, the work of artists from across the globe. They are so vibrant and varied in design – some filling walls five storeys high – that many visitors come to Shoreditch simply to see and admire the brilliant artwork.

Street art in Shoreditch.

For centuries these two neighbourhoods have accommodated huge waves of immigrants, and it is here that new settlers have often lived in abject poverty. French Huguenots skilled in silk weaving, precision tool making, printing and engraving arrived here in 1685 having fled France after religious persecution, the Irish came to work on the construction of the canals and railways in the early 1800s and, later, many Jews from Poland and Russia settled in the district having escaped terrible oppression in Eastern Europe. Since then Shoreditch and Hoxton has seen a great influx of people from the Asian subcontinent, especially Bangladesh, and their golden mile of restaurants on Brick Lane is one of East London's best-known attractions, enticing visitors from every corner of the globe. Interestingly, each new group has brought its customs and religious practices to the neighbourhood's streets, and this has led to the 'Neuve Eglise', the eighteenth-century French Huguenot church on Brick Lane, being converted not once but twice, first into a synagogue and then a mosque.

So many of the buildings one passes in Shoreditch and Hoxton are associated with trades that characterised the area in former times; the massive Truman brewery with its towering chimney dominates the western end of Brick Lane, and printworks, furniture showrooms, warehouses, factories and buildings associated with the clothing and tobacco industries are spread throughout the districts. Some have been converted into office space, while others have become residential accommodation, or even a museum, theatre or nightclub. The splendid Shoreditch Magistrates' Court is now the five-star luxury Courthouse Hotel, Shoreditch, while the chapel of the former Central Foundation School for Girls houses Galvin la Chappelle, one of London's highly reputed Michelin star restaurants. Gainsborough (film) Studios' former canal-side premises are now filled with apartments, the giant sculptured head of Alfred Hitchcock in its grounds being the only clue to its previous incarnation.

Over the years these neighbourhoods have gone through periods of appalling poverty and overcrowding and for much of the nineteenth century they were notorious for their tenement and slum areas, especially Old Nichol on the boundary between Shoreditch and Bethnal Green. Philanthropists and social reformers such as George Peabody and Charles Booth worked hard to improve the lot of the disadvantaged and needy and to raise awareness about their plight. Peabody provided funds for affordable homes for the decent working poor to be built in Commercial Street while Booth wrote books, published reports, and lobbied government in the hope of influencing policy. Fortunately their labours were not in vain and brought positive results. In the late 1890s the newly formed London County Council (LCC) demolished the Old Nichol and approved the construction of the Boundary Estate, London's, and possibly the world's, very first council estate, which became a template for other local authorities to follow.

Throughout the nineteenth century Shoreditch and Hoxton's appearance regularly changed due to the building of the Regent's Canal, the newly constructed railways with their viaducts and multitude of arches and the building of wide thoroughfares such as Great Eastern Street. The furniture industry took over the street scene with its huge warehouses, showrooms and factories, and smaller family-run workshops filled the area's warren of narrow streets. South Shoreditch became renowned for supplying every type of furniture both at home and overseas and employed large numbers in its trade. However, the Second World War had a great impact on the industry from which it never really recovered. Many buildings were destroyed or damaged, and the district became subject to competition from UK manufacturers outside the area and from growing rival imports. Ultimately by the late 1900s the furniture trade here had to all intents and purposes collapsed.

This was the point when many of the area's decaying and derelict buildings were snapped up by people like Californian artist Dennis Severs who went on to renovate an eighteenth-century Huguenot house on Folgate Street, and contemporary artists looking for cheap studios and digs. Since that time the entire district has undergone enormous urban renewal with loft apartments and luxury co-working space becoming the norm and high-rise towers erected matching those in the City of London. Shoreditch and Hoxton continue to evolve and as such are always fascinating places to visit. Their mix of old and new buildings, their many clubs, hotels, bars, shops, restaurants, pubs and live music venues, and their atmosphere of cool living is on display everywhere. Night-time here is so very vibrant with streets crammed full of people enjoying themselves. Undoubtedly trendy and unconventional yet full of history Shoreditch and Hoxton are certainly worth exploring and I hope that you, like me, will appreciate the areas' great urban scene and truly magical vibes.

How to use this book

In accordance with the 50 Buildings series, the buildings appear in chronological order according to the time of their original construction. The accompanying map identifies each building by a number that corresponds to the numbers used in the text. Website information for buildings that are open to the public is provided at the end of each chapter.

Please note

Many of the buildings within the book appear on English Heritage's Register of Listed Buildings, a designation that recognises historic and/or architectural significance. This 'listed status' (ranging from the top Grade I, through II* to II) necessitates strict planning rules which helps to prevent essential features of the buildings from being lost, preserving them for future generations.

The 50 Buildings

1. Church of St Leonard, No. 119 Shoreditch High Street, E1

Occupying a substantial and commanding site at the junction of Shoreditch High Street and Old Street, the Church of St. Leonard is one of Shoreditch's most prominent landmarks. Familiarly known as Shoreditch Church, it sits on, Ermine Street, the Roman road that stretched between London, Lincoln and York. The church's grand portico, supported by four enormous Tuscan columns, and its distinctive tall and narrow steeple, 192 feet (60 metres) high, make the church highly visible. It is particularly well known because of its association with the children's nursery rhyme *Oranges and Lemons*, in the lines:

When will you pay me?
Say the bells at Old Bailey
When I grow rich,
Say the bells of Shoreditch …

St Leonard's Church, Shoreditch.

The present church was built in 1736 and is dedicated to St Leonard, the sixth-century patron saint of prisoners. It was designed by the famous Georgian architect George Dance the Elder (1695–1768), surveyor to the Corporation of London and renowned for his work on Mansion House. Shoreditch Church, built in the classical style, is known to have replaced churches that stood here from the late twelfth century and throughout the medieval period. Its façade is constructed of Portland stone while its sides and rear are red brick. St Leonard's still retains a number of original features including its early eighteenth-century font, pulpit and beautiful mahogany Bridge organ.

In the late 1500s the church became known as the 'actor's church' as many of its parishioners, including the playwright and actor William Shakespeare, were employed in the neighbourhood in James Burbage's Theatre and Curtain playhouses. Today, visitors to the church will see a memorial plaque to these actors in the church entrance. Other notable people associated with St Leonard's include the scientist and surgeon James Parkinson, buried here in 1824 and after

St Leonard's Church, Shoreditch.

Nave of St Leonard's Church, Shoreditch. (SAINT Church)

whom Parkinson's Disease is named, and the Romantic poet John Keats, who was baptised in the church in 1795.

For some time the church was on the English Heritage 'Buildings at Risk' register but with funding from several organisations including the National Heritage Lottery, it was able to carry out structural restoration, which has allowed Shoreditch Church to return to its former splendour.

Stations: Shoreditch High Street, Hoxton, Old Street
www.saint.church/shoreditch/

2. Museum of the Home, No. 136 Kingsland Road, E2

Built as almshouses for pensioners in 1714–15, this beautiful Grade I listed building is nowadays a museum and specialises in everything pertaining to the domestic home. The museum's collection is vast and consists primarily of furniture but also wallpaper and textile samples, glass and tableware, ceramics, paintings, ornaments, audio and oral histories and a variety of objects that highlight domestic life since the 1600s. When the London County Council purchased the building in the early 1900s it established it as a museum of furniture and woodwork, acting as a reference resource for people working in the local cabinetmaking and furniture trade. However, in the 1930s the museum decided to focus more on the history of domestic life to show the various changes in society, style and taste over the centuries and demonstrate furnishings, social and economic trends. A series of period rooms set in chronological order were constructed along the entire length of the building, showing how living spaces had evolved and changed over time. This remained the museum's permanent display until the late 1990s when a further wing was built, and rooms from the twentieth century were added. The Geffrye Museum as it was then known (named after the eighteenth-century benefactor of the original almshouses) closed for refurbishment in 2018 and reopened three years later following an £18 million development project. At this point it was renamed the Museum of the Home. Now with much greater exhibition and public space the museum has opened up its basement as The Home Galleries and

Above: The Museum of the Home.

Right: Drawing room in the Museum of the Home. (Museum of the Home)

has built an entirely new entrance facing directly on to Hoxton Overground station. The museum has additionally benefited from a learning pavilion, reference libraries, a café and shop. It offers many activities for children and families and is free to visit, opening Tuesday to Sunday between 10.00 and 17.00.

When the almshouses were first built they housed about fifty poor pensioners who were each given an unfurnished room, six bags of coal and a pension of £6 annually. The institution was administered by the Ironmongers' Company and there were four staff, including a chaplain and a matron living on site.

Station: Hoxton
www.museumofthehome.org.uk

3. Hoxton Square, N1

Hoxton Square was the first garden square to be built in East London in the latter part of the seventeenth century. It was an upmarket housing development and became immediately fashionable (in keeping with St James's Square, constructed in London's West End following the Great Fire of London in 1666) appealing to the wealthy. The houses, completed by the 1720s, were built around an attractive central garden with several streets leading into the square around its sides. Surprisingly, the layout of the streets has changed little in 300 years and anyone entering Hoxton Square now has the distinct feeling of walking into an intimate space, almost an oasis cut off from the surrounding busy urban scene.

None of the square's early houses remain in their entirety, although the Grade II listed No. 32 is thought to be possibly from the late seventeenth century. Most buildings here today are brick-built and at least four to five storeys high. Although many are architecturally different in style, they are generally uniform in size and blend well together. The majority of them were built in the mid-to-late 1800s, some then used as commercial warehouses, others for industrial, religious or residential purposes. At this time Hoxton was the thriving centre of the furniture industry and many of the front gardens of the square's houses were adapted for use as small workshops, but these have long since disappeared.

Below left: No. 10 Hoxton Square.

Below right: White Cube Building, Hoxton Square.

No. 32 Hoxton Square.

As the century drew to a close Hoxton became a villainous area with great poverty and overcrowding, with Charles Booth, the social reformer, describing it 'as the leading criminal quarter of London…' Certainly, the square had by now lost its original high-end status and the twentieth century saw it become mainly an area of light industry. The 1990s saw a complete reversal of its fortunes when developers transformed the square into a buzzing district full of media companies, bars and restaurants. Once the art dealer Jay Jopling established his White Cube art gallery here in 2002, showcasing the work of Young British Artists (YBAs) such as Damien Hirst and Tracey Emin, the square's future was assured. Nowadays, Hoxton Square is one of east London's most popular night-time venues.

Stations: Hoxton, Old Street

4. Dennis Severs' House, No. 18 Folgate Street, E1

A visit to Dennis Severs' House is an utterly unforgettable experience, almost a flight of fancy for any visitor fortunate enough to enter the Californian artist's house. Severs (1948–99), moved to London in the 1960s and bought his house in Folgate Street in 1979 at a time when the entire area was not only shabby but run-down and practically derelict. His artistic temperament together with a real appreciation for the past saw him spend many hours perusing stalls at local markets in search of objects that would express the life and activities that had occurred within the walls of his house in the eighteenth and nineteenth centuries. So that he could best gauge the atmosphere and soul of his home he slept in each of the ten rooms within the house, taking a candle, mattress and chamber pot with him as he went.

Above left: Dennis Severs' House.

Above right: Drawing room, Dennis Severs' House. (Lucinda Douglas Menzies)

Left: Upstairs bedroom, Dennis Severs' House. (Lucinda Douglas Menzies)

Part of a Georgian terrace, the house was built in the 1720s and located in the centre of a Huguenot community of silk weavers. Severs became so immersed in the restoration and refurbishment of his home that he invented as former tenants the Jervis's, a family of silk weavers, and went about adapting each room to a different period of their occupancy. Using sound effects, candles and smells to conjure up moods and atmosphere, he created stories of their family life, making each room look as if in use, and by theatrical touches such as half-eaten food he cleverly invoked the idea that members of the family had only just left that particular space. Severs himself described his home as 'a still life drama' and thought of it not as a museum but more of an exhibition experience. He was certainly a man of great passion intent on bringing to life the social history of the East End through his own perception of time gone by. Undoubtedly eccentric, Severs was also very talented as a visit to the house will show. Sadly, he died in 1999 but his work can still be appreciated as the house, now owned by the Spitalfields Trust, is open to the public from Thursday to Sunday each week.

Stations: Liverpool Street, Shoreditch High Street
www.dennisevershouse.co.uk

5. Fournier Street – Gilbert & George, E1

Fournier Street was constructed in the 1720s as a street of thirty-four merchants' houses. It is a narrow road that sits between Spitalfields and Brick Lane and today has a charming air of utter gentility. From the start these houses stood out from others in the locale as they were built to a superior standard, embellished with sash windows, shutters and ornamental drain heads. Some even displayed wooden spools outside showing their connection with the weavers who ultimately worked and lived in the houses in the eighteenth century. The interiors were of high quality too, with wooden-panelled rooms and intricately carved mahogany stairwells. The houses soon became home to the recently arrived French Huguenot weavers. Built on four floors, the ground floor of the townhouse acted as a showroom for the weavers' finished products, while the floors above provided family living quarters and workshops in the attic. Here, windows extended along the width of the house to provide the necessary light required by the weavers when working the looms. If you walk along Fournier Street today these windows are still very much in evidence.

Over the years the street became run-down, and its houses were divided up, frequently occupied by several families. Continuous waves of immigrants and refugees (Irish, Jewish – from Russia and Poland – West Indian and Bangladeshi) settled here and initially many were employed in the textile industry. Nowadays residents work in a range of industries, from restaurants and hospitality to the arts, acting, the music world and law, as well as finance and technology. The area

Above left: Decorative porch, Fournier Street.

Above right: Gilbert & George's home, Fournier Street.

Left: Attic workrooms, Fournier Street.

The Main Gallery within The Gilbert & George Centre.

has also attracted artists such as the celebrated duo Gilbert & George, who have lived here since the late 1960s.

At that time the street was very shabby and neglected but Gilbert & George have meticulously restored two houses along the street and have been copied by others since, making Fournier Street what it is today. Most recently the artists have opened The Gilbert & George Centre in nearby Heneage Street. It is filled with their art, which is displayed in several stunning gallery spaces around the building.

Stations: Liverpool Street, Aldgate East

6. Brick Lane and Beigel Bake, E1

Brick Lane has been in existence since the fifteenth century when it was surrounded by fields. Initially known as Whitechapel Lane, its name later changed to Brick Lane to reflect the nature of the industry that had grown up here due to an abundant supply of clay deposits in the vicinity.

Right in the centre of London's East End, Brick Lane has been home to immigrants for hundreds of years. Each wave of new arrivals has added to the character of the street, as well as introducing new trades, shops and cuisine. The street names today are written in both English and Bengali script, recognising the current mix of residents of the area, and an imposing colourful archway marking the entrance to 'Banglatown' sits at the southern end of the street. When the Bengalis settled here in the 1970s many were involved in the textile industry, employed in squalid workshops cutting materials, trimming and buttonholing garments but since the late twentieth century

Above: Street scene, Brick Lane.

Left: Street signage, Brick Lane.

the main employment is in the restaurant trade. Brick Lane today is lined with curry houses, which have become internationally renowned. So much so that it is said that no stay in London is complete without a visit to this almost mile-long street.

Beigel Bake at No. 159 Brick Lane was opened fifty years ago at a time when there was still a sizeable Jewish population living in Shoreditch and the East End. Although their population has since dwindled here, the bakery has remained a major feature of the street, opening twenty-four hours a day, seven days a week. Throngs of visitors arrive here daily to sample Beigel Bake's north European Jewish fare, especially its awesome beigels, salt beef sandwiches and legendary desserts. However, the bakery is not somewhere to come for a relaxing meal with

Beigel Bake, Brick Lane.

waiter service. You are most likely to have to queue on the street before ordering, but the wait is more than worth it as everything is freshly prepared, of the highest quality, cheap and service is fast. The bakery has an enormous turnover of beigels and claims to produce more than 7,000 of them each day.

Station: Shoreditch High Street

7. Nos 3 and 5 Club Row, E1

Dating to 1764–65, these three-storey houses were built for use by weavers serving the local silk industry and are excellent examples of housing constructed for this distinct purpose. They were constructed in brown stock brick and built as workshop tenement houses, originally part of a larger group. The exterior shape of the properties with their segmental arched windows was designed to ensure the weavers' workshops received sufficient light for the work in hand. In the eighteenth century these buildings could be found all over the district but nowadays such houses are a rarity and are all the more important historically as a result. It is believed that they were perhaps the first purpose-built housing to both fulfil the requirements of a particular industry and provide domestic accommodation.

Over the years Nos 3 and 5 Club Row have undergone many changes, with ground-floor shopfronts added in the nineteenth century. In its time, No. 3 has been home to a bird dealer, a handbag manufacturer, and today it is in residential

Nos 3 and 5 Club Row.

use. No. 5 has also had many uses. In the late 1800s it was a coffee room and by the mid-twentieth century cane furniture was manufactured here. Now the building has mixed usage – with commercial and residential occupants.

Station: Shoreditch High Street

8. Jamme Masjid Mosque, No. 59 Brick Lane, E1

If only this building could talk, for it has the most fascinating history and has acted as the religious heart of the community for almost 300 years. Today, it is a sacred hub for its Muslim worshippers and known as the Jamme Masjid Mosque, but the building began life in the 1740s as a French Protestant chapel, the Neuve Eglise, when it served a large Huguenot Protestant congregation. After the Huguenots moved away from the district in the nineteenth century the church was converted into a synagogue for the area's new Jewish immigrants and remodelled by the Maples furniture company in the late 1890s. The Great Synagogue as it was known became the religious centre and focal point for the new Russian and Polish Jewish settlers who had fled from oppression and persecution in their own countries. In the ensuing years the Jewish community living beside the synagogue on Brick Lane flourished and the neighbourhood was characterised by its Jewish shops, factories, workshops and homes. After the Second World War much of the Jewish population moved away to other parts of London and a new wave of immigrants from Bangladesh replaced them. In 1976 the former synagogue was transformed into a mosque to serve its now Muslim congregation. Once again modifications and alterations were made to the building. With each change of religion the building gained or lost furniture and galleries and some of its rooms have been adapted for different purposes, but the structure remained, in essence, the same as it was when first built.

On account of its architectural merit and historical significance the Jamme Masjid Mosque is now a Grade II* listed building, which means that repairs must be carried out using original materials and any proposed alterations must be approved by English Heritage before work can go ahead. The mosque is a real landmark on Brick Lane with its tall free-standing minaret. Round the corner on Fournier Street take time to look at the sundial in the building's pediment, which contains the date 1743, as well as the maxim 'UMBRA SUMUS' – meaning 'we are but shadows'. A poignant and aptly worded statement.

Stations: Liverpool Street, Aldgate East
www.bricklanejammemasjid.org.uk

Right: Jamme Masjid Mosque, Brick Lane.

Below: Sundial on mosque wall, Fournier Street.

9. The Old Truman Brewery, Brick Lane, E1

When the Truman brewery ceased trading in the late 1980s its buildings were reinvented as an exciting arts hub filled with galleries, shops and exhibition space. It is now one of the most visited and popular venues in Shoreditch, receiving a constant flow of visitors who come to experience its many and varied spaces filled with creative art, food stalls, shops, bars, cafés and restaurants.

The brewery was initially known as the Black Eagle Brewery and its black eagle crest is still visible around its present boundary. Established in the 1660s, Joseph Truman bought the brewery in 1679. After his death in the 1720s the family carried on the business until Sampson Hanbury became a partner in 1780 and subsequently ran the company. He was later joined by his nephew Thomas Foxwell Buxton and in the early 1800s the highly successful brewery became known as Truman, Hanbury, Buxton & Co. Besides being a brewer, Thomas Foxwell Buxton was also a Member of Parliament (MP), a philanthropist and an ardent abolitionist of the slave trade. His many lifetime achievements are commemorated in an English Heritage blue plaque on his former home, the Director's House in Brick Lane, as well as memorials found in Westminster Abbey and Victoria Tower Gardens (the latter consisting of an extremely ornate Victorian drinking fountain).

Clock tower and chimney, Old Truman Brewery.

Above: Director's House, Old Truman Brewery.

Right: Truman brewery buildings, Brick Lane.

The Truman brewery was an extensive estate and included the brewmaster's and engineer's houses, as well as stables and a vat house (now all Grade II listed). The Director's House today is designated Grade II* as it is both an excellent example of an eighteenth-century townhouse and domestic home, as well as being the company's main headquarters. The entire complex is a marvellous example of eighteenth- to twentieth-century brewery buildings, and one rarely found elsewhere.

Most recently planning permission has been granted to convert part of the former brewery into an office and shopping centre. If the development goes ahead, it is likely to result in the expulsion of many of the small businesses currently trading on the site and for this reason the proposal has met with great opposition and remains a highly contentious project.

Station: Shoreditch High Street
www.trumanbrewery.com

10. Eagle Tavern & Former Grecian Theatre, No. 2 Shepherdess Walk, N1

The present pub dates to 1900 and is a popular haunt of visitors to Shoreditch. Nowadays it is a much smaller and less well-known establishment than it was in times gone by, making it hard to imagine the immense size and grandeur of the original Eagle tavern during its prime in the nineteenth century.

In fact, the site had been used for entertainment since the mid-1700s, initially as the Shepherd and Shepherdess Tea Garden and from the 1820s as the Eagle tavern. From the early 1800s it functioned not only as a tavern but also as a music hall-cum-theatre with a pavilion in the grounds known as the Grecian Saloon. Saloon theatres were fashionable at the time and attracted audiences that liked to see dramatic turns while drinking and smoking. The Grecian Saloon turned into the Grecian Theatre and frequently underwent alteration until being entirely rebuilt in 1877 – at which point it could seat a crowd of 4,000. Unfortunately, many of its patrons were rowdy and badly behaved, which led to a downturn in the Eagle's reputation and resulted

The Eagle public house.

in the premises changing hands. Under its new tenant, the Salvation Army, the establishment became far more virtuous but by the dawn of the twentieth century the Salvation Army had left the site and the Eagle and Grecian buildings were then demolished. A new, much smaller pub was erected in their place.

During its heyday the Eagle and Grecian had been associated with many famous names. Here the singer and entertainer Marie Lloyd made her debut in 1885 and launched her very successful career as a music hall artiste. The Eagle was also the subject of a short essay in Charles Dickens' *Sketches by Boz*, where he described the music hall, the orchestra and audience. All manner of entertainment took place here ranging from musical works and opera, wrestling, stick fights and fireworks to equestrian performances, dancing and even balloon ascents.

The Eagle is reputed to have inspired the nursery rhyme 'Pop Goes the Weasel' with its opening lines: 'Up and down the City Road, In and out the Eagle…', a song about pawning items to pay for one's entertainment in the tavern!

Station: Old Street
www.theeaglehoxton.co.uk

11. Former Aske's Almhouses and London College of Furniture, Pitfield Street, N1.

Today the building contains forty apartments and is known as Hoffman Square, having been converted in 2001 from its previous use as the London College of Furniture. It is a fine Grade II listed stone and brick building with a central stone tetrastyle portico of the Doric order. Two storeys high, it has an attractive frieze carved with laurel wreaths and there are stone plaques on either side of the entrance door containing the history of the Aske charity.

The structure owes its roots to a wealthy merchant and member of the Haberdashers' Company, Robert Aske (1619–89), who bequeathed a sum of £20,000 on his death to the livery company to establish an almshouse for twenty poor single freemen of the company and a school for twenty poor boys. The company purchased 21 acres of land and commissioned Robert Hooke (1635–1703), a contemporary of Sir Christopher Wren, to design the buildings. By 1695 both the school and almshouses were open. The grand central block housed the schoolrooms and chapel and the almshouses, each with ten apartments, were placed in detached terraces on either side of the main building. The Haberdashers' Company managed the buildings, employing domestic and pastoral staff, as well as a chaplain, steward, butler, porter and cooks.

By 1822 the school buildings were in a state of disrepair. Shortly afterwards they were pulled down and rebuilt in the Greek Regency style by D. R. Roper (*c.* 1773–1855). The almshouses were closed fifty years later, and the buildings demolished. The school expanded once again, now accommodating 300 boys and 300 girls.

Above: Former Museum of Furniture, Pitfield Street.

Left: Entrance to former Museum of Furniture, Pitfield Street.

In 1898 the schools moved out of London and the London County Council (LCC) took over the site. The building first became the Shoreditch Technical Institute, then Shoreditch College and finally in 1964 the London College of Furniture.

The latter, in addition to its courses on furniture, offered a far greater range of subjects than had previously been taught. Students studied musical instrument making, interior design, soft furnishings and textiles, creative crafts and design for disability, and the college was highly respected. It remained here until 1992 when it became part of London Guildhall, then London Metropolitan University.

Station: Old Street

12. Church of St John the Baptist, Pitfield Street, N1

Constructed between 1824 and 1826, the church was built as a chapel of ease to St Leonard's Shoreditch, but within only a short time it became established as an independent parish church. It was a period of huge growth in Hoxton and Shoreditch and the need for a new church to serve the ever-growing population was fortunately recognised by the religious authorities. Initially it was the only parish church serving Hoxton and funding for the building (£15,394) came via the Church Building Commissioners. The architect Francis Edwards (1784–1857), a pupil of Sir John Soane's in his Lincoln's Inn Fields offices, was highly respected in London where he specialised in neoclassical architecture.

Hoxton's St John the Baptist Church is a fine example of a 'Commissioners' church, although unusually large. Built in the classical style, it has an impressive tower at its west end that begins as a square and then extends upwards into two circular tiers finishing with a stone cupola. The main entranceway beneath it is flanked by two enormous Ionic columns and there is an impressive horizontal band between the upper and lower windows stretching around the entire building. The church now carries Grade II* listing largely because it has retained its original undamaged floor plan and because its gallery seating has remained intact (even though the doors to the pews are no longer in situ). Signs of its Victorian and Edwardian restorations are still evident, as well as the splendid redecoration carried out in the early 1900s, the work of Joseph Arthur Reeve (1850–1915). Reeve's ceiling ornamentation with its angels of the Apocalypse is one of the

St John the Baptist Church.

Above: St John the Baptist Church.

Left: Organ and upstairs gallery, St John the Baptist Church.

church's greatest features and is highly acclaimed as a wonderful example of decorative arrangement of the early twentieth century.

Today the congregation is much smaller than in the nineteenth century, yet the church continues to administer to the needs of those living in the somewhat poor inner-city neighbourhood. In such a way it continues work first begun two centuries ago and aims to be 'a beacon of hope for Hoxton'.

Stations: Hoxton, Old Street
www.stjohnshoxton.org.uk

13. Hoxton Hall, No. 130 Hoxton Street, N1

Hoxton Hall has been operating from this site since 1863 and is undoubtedly one of Hoxton's hidden treasures. Built in a horseshoe shape, it is a purpose-built Victorian music hall with galleries on three sides and is one of few surviving halls of its type in the country. The building has always served the working classes and particularly the local community. From its launch it provided a great variety of entertainment – circus turns, music and drama – and even those from the poorest backgrounds could afford its prices. Throughout its lifetime Hoxton Hall has had many uses including periods spent as a women's club, a temperance society, and in the 1960s the artists Gilbert and George ran art classes here.

During the Second World War local resident May Scott introduced a host of activities which resulted in Hoxton Hall becoming the vibrant hub of the local community. Her legacy continues today with young and old able to access a fantastic programme of cultural events including gigs, theatre, dance, performance, circus and pantomime – much in the style of the original music hall. Nowadays the centre runs excellent youth programmes, has its own recording studio and its many varied spaces are available for hire. Its small and wonderfully

Above left: Hoxton Hall Auditorium. (Hoxton Hall)

Above right: Gothic Opera's 'Rip Van Winkle' at Hoxton Hall. (Hoxton Hall)

Hoxton Hall's 'Strictly Hoxton' event. (Sean Pollock)

intimate auditorium has a magical atmosphere and anyone visiting the building will immediately understand why it has Grade II* listing.

Station: Hoxton
www.hoxtonhall.co.uk

14. Former Church of St Michael and All Angels, Mark Street, EC2

The church was the first major ecclesiastical project of the architect James Brooks (1825–1901) in London and considered by many to be his greatest work. Designed in 1863 in the Victorian Gothic style and completed two years later, the Church of St Michael and All Angels was immediately hailed for its monumental size and for its many splendid internal and external features. Indeed the church still stands out for its wonderful polychrome brickwork – yellow brick with red and blue brick bands – and is renowned for its octagonal stone bell turret, its lancet and plate tracery windows and exquisite Clayton and Bell east window. Built for a congregation of 1,000 worshippers, the church, along with its neighbouring vicarage, school and the Convent of St Mary at the Cross, served the local population for around 100 years and the site was recognised as a key landmark in Shoreditch. Nonetheless, after the Second World War the number of churchgoers fell, and this led to the church closing in 1964.

Former St Michael's and All Angels Church.

After its deconsecration the church was occupied by a salvage, architectural and antiques business that filled the church nave and the outside yard with its enormous collection of rescued artefacts including antique furniture, fireplaces, chimneypieces, lighting and mirrors. It was a great favourite with both trade visitors and tourists alike, who visited the former church to browse and buy. However, after many years occupancy the antique emporium moved out of the building in 2019, leaving the church empty once again.

This gave the owners, Mark Street Depository Ltd, the opportunity to restore and repurpose the former church and its outside space for office use. They commissioned Trehearn Architects, who proposed two intercommunicating buildings, connecting the former church with a new state-of-the-art building placed over the old yard facing Leonard Street. Being a Grade I listed building meant that alterations to the fabric of the church would be limited so only a partial mezzanine floor has been planned within the revamped building. The project is now well underway, and it will be of great interest to see how the buildings complement one another when the work is finally completed.

Stations: Old Street, Shoreditch High Street

15. Nos 91–101 Worship Street, EC2

The socialist and architect Philip Webb (1831–1915) designed this terrace of affordable workshops and living space in 1862 – almost revolutionary for the time as it incorporated artisan homes each with its own studio and shop. In the 1850s Webb had been a pupil of the great ecclesiastical and Gothic architect G. E. Street (responsible for the Royal Courts of Justice in the Strand) and it was at his practice that he met fellow designer, poet and artist William Morris (1834–96). The two men became not only great friends but also shared many of the same political and aesthetic beliefs, especially ideas about decorative and fine arts. They regarded vernacular architecture, by which they meant traditional style, buildings made to last, work by traditional skilled craftsmen and the use of sound local materials, to be the way forward. These values, together with their opposition to production by mass means, were fundamental in the Arts and Crafts movement that the men spearheaded. Throughout their lives Webb and Morris maintained a very close working relationship. Webb not only designed Morris's Bexleyheath home, The Red House, but later became a partner in his friend's firm, Morris and Co. The two also co-founded the Society for the Protection of Ancient Buildings in 1877.

Nos 91–101 Worship Street today is a rather down-at-heel block, but its architecture is still a marvellous example of the Arts and Crafts style. The houses are all listed Grade II* on account of their architectural design best demonstrated by the steeply pitched roofs, Gothic-style pointed window arches and use of plain stock brick, wood and handmade clay roof tiles. Each property bears a shop at ground level where the artisan's crafts could be sold, a studio in the basement and accommodation on three floors above for the family to live. It was envisaged that by incorporating work and home life in the same premises costs would be kept down

Nos 91–101 Worship Street.

and the artisans would be able to support one another. Although originally used for this purpose, the terrace is now split up into single floors and Webb's original intention of craftsmen living upstairs and working below has sadly vanished.

Stations: Liverpool Street, Old Street, Shoreditch High Street

16. Nos 49–50 Eagle Wharf Road, N1 (now Holborn Studios)

Holborn Studios is a venue known worldwide for its list of celebrities who have taken part in photoshoots within its maze of Victorian warehouses. Artists, photographers and celebrities including Madonna, Kate Moss, David Bowie, Helen Mirren, Shirley Bassey, Frankie Dettori, James Corden, Bill Bailey and even former Prime Minister Margaret Thatcher have all crossed the studio's threshold to attend photo sessions and many famous film moments have been captured here. Holborn Studios is one of the greatest photographic studio complexes in Europe today and is made up of eight photographic and film studio spaces, which are used for photoshoots, filming and fashion shoots and also hired for parties, weddings, events and conferences.

Interestingly, the building's early life was dominated by engineering rather than photography. In 1841 it became the foundry of one of England's most important

Below left: Holborn Studios Courtyard, Eagle Wharf Road. (Holborn Studios)

Below right: View of Holborn Studios from Regent's Canal. (Holborn Studios)

Holborn Studios.
(Holborn Studios)

and esteemed structural iron founders, Henry Grissell (1817–83) for his company, The Regent's Canal Iron Works operating on the site until 1866. Grissell's firm was instrumental in building railway bridges in London, railings for Buckingham Palace and many of the cast-iron floors and roofs at the Houses of Parliament. His company was also responsible for the decorative and intricate cast-iron façades of the Royal Opera House's Floral Hall in Covent Garden. Situated beside the canal, the foundry was ideally placed to receive raw materials and later to ship out the finished products from its lay-by on the canal outside the ironworks.

For nearly ten years Holborn Studios' premises had been threatened with closure and plans to replace the studios with a mixed use residential and commercial development were initially approved by the local council. However, after a High Court battle the proposed demolition of the iconic site was ruled unlawful and quashed by the High Court in 2020. This decision has allowed the company to continue its vital role in the regeneration of the area, to remain a major local employer, as well as a thriving media centre. Holborn Studios is regarded by many in the creative community to be in the words of fashion photographer Helmut Newton, the 'Abbey Road of Photography'.

Stations: Old Street, Angel, Essex Road
www.holbornstudios.com

17. Relief Office, St Leonard's Hospital, Hoxton Street and Kingsland Road, N1

Built in 1777 as the St Leonard Shoreditch Workhouse, the building was replaced in the 1860s by a new workhouse, which later became known as St Leonard's Hospital. The original Victorian workhouse was renowned for its harsh rules and work conditions, and men, women and their children were kept segregated. It was certainly the most undesirable place to live and was purposely designed to be such so that only paupers and the totally destitute would be housed within its walls.

Inmates included the infirm, who initially lived alongside those who were healthy, but in 1872 an infirmary was constructed for the sick beside the new workhouse along with a dispensary and later a nurse's home, laundry and separate receiving blocks for men and women.

Over time many of the buildings have disappeared but the hospital's frontage on Kingsland Road with its impressive carved stonework and decorative iron cresting has survived and carries Grade II listing. It was part of the original nineteenth-century workhouse and built in the French Second Empire style. Four storeys high, it has an additional attic floor with tall mansards and patterned slate coverings, as well as a basement, and is easy identifiable for its red-brick and Portland stone exterior. This part of the hospital sits adjacent to the Church of St Columba (now the Christ Apostolic Church) and the two buildings together have become recognised as a major local landmark.

In total contrast to its Kingsland Road frontage the hospital's Hoxton Street façade is Italianate in design. It is impossible to miss as it bears a prominent inscription in capital letters beneath its central first-floor pediment that reads: 'St Leonard – 1863 – Shoreditch – Offices for the Relief of the Poor'. Today, this

St Leonard's Hospital, Kingsland Road.

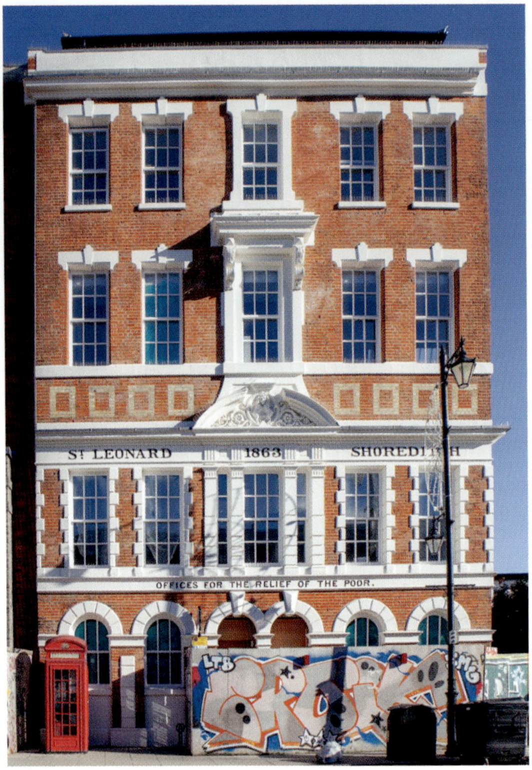

St Leonard's Hospital Offices for the Relief of the Poor, Hoxton Street.

façade is the only part of the original building to survive, and the hospital now functions as a primary care centre.

In the early nineteenth century the surgeon James Parkinson (1755–1824) worked at St Leonard's and established a separate fever block here. It was Parkinson who described the shaking palsy, a condition that we now refer to as 'Parkinson's Disease'.

Station: Hoxton

18. Church of St Monica, and the Priory of the Augustinian Friars, Hoxton Square, N1

Facing the gardens of Hoxton Square, St Monica's Church instantly catches the eye due to its narrow frontage, huge buttresses and slender bellcote surmounting the church's superb Gothic Perpendicular west window. St Monica's, a Catholic church, was designed by Edward Welby Pugin (1834–75), the eldest son of the celebrated architect of the Houses of Parliament, Augustus Welby Pugin, and was built on a small budget. Nonetheless, it contains a host of interesting features and is a great tribute to Edward Pugin's architectural skill.

St Monica's RC Church, Hoxton Square.

The church was opened in the mid-1860s as a mission church along with the Priory of Augustinian Friars. Linked to one another, the buildings, constructed of stock brick and stone dressings, form a distinctive architectural group on the north side of the square.

Originally a primary school was built alongside the church and priory, also to Pugin's design, but in the 1970s the school and land were sold off and subsequently a new primary school has replaced it a little further along the north side of the square.

The interior of the church is quite unexpected; light and lofty, it boasts a timber ceiling supported by an arcade of wooden pillars, and the altar and reredos are also made of wood. Although this was not Pugin's normal style, the result is quite splendid. Presumably his reason for working with timber was because Hoxton at the time was a major furniture making centre and so he was able to employ highly skilled woodworkers from the area's furniture trade.

On either side of the nave the twelve stations of the cross light up the walls and the beautiful stained-glass east window portraying St Monica (replaced following war damage) illuminates the entire building. The church underwent a major restoration in 2013 at which time fabulous Gothic-inspired frescoes containing Latin inscriptions and floral decorations designed by Pugin were revealed beside the gilded altar.

St Monica's RC Church, Hoxton Square.

Chancel and rose window, St Monica's RC Church, Hoxton Square.

St Monica's has always been at the heart of the local Catholic community, which it continues to serve actively. Mass is celebrated here daily, and the church runs many activities including youth groups for its congregation.

Stations: Old Street, Shoreditch High Street, Hoxton
https://parish.rcdow.org.uk/hoxton/

19. Former Peabody Housing, Nos 135–153 Commercial Street, E1

The buildings that straddle the junction of Commercial Street and Folgate Street are nowadays known as The Cloisters and contain apartments in private ownership. Located in the very heart of Shoreditch so close to the City of London, and only moments away from a huge selection of bars, cafés, clubs and restaurants, the flats are highly sought after and do not come cheap. So it is ironic to discover that these apartments were initially built in 1864 as a philanthropic social housing project for

London by the newly founded Peabody Trust. Pioneered by American-born George Peabody (1795–1869), they were built to house poor but respectable Londoners at a time when the East End was vastly overcrowded, full of substandard housing and where families were often squeezed into one room of a house. The capital saw such a population explosion in the 1800s that many of the decent working poor were unable to afford homes despite being in regular and salaried employment.

Peabody, a wealthy merchant banker, settled in London in 1837 and was so moved by the terrible destitution and poverty he saw around him that he founded the Peabody Trust in 1862 to ameliorate the condition of the poor. The site in Commercial Street was designed by H. A. Darbyshire, who subsequently became the trust's main architect. Peabody's initial development consisted of two five-storey buildings that met at the angled corner of Commercial Street and Folgate Street. The block on Commercial Street had retail outlets at ground floor level, with a five-room maisonette behind the shop and the premises were let out at market rates. The rent for the flats was kept purposely low and residents leased between one and three rooms. Although basic, the accommodation was well-built

Former Peabody Buildings, Commercial and Folgate streets.

Shops in former Peabody Buildings, Commercial Street.

and contained sanitation. Moreover, it had the benefit of communal drying rooms, laundries and bathrooms on the top floor.

On his death in 1869 Peabody was honoured with a funeral and burial in Westminster Abbey. However, instructions in his will requested that his body be returned to his hometown of Danvers, Massachusetts, which then renamed itself Peabody in commemoration of the great man.

Station: Shoreditch High Street, Liverpool Street

20. Former Church of St Columba, Kingsland Road, E2 (now Christ Apostolic Church)

One cannot fail to be impressed by the fine architecture and magnitude of St Columba's Church sitting at the junction of Kingsland Road and Nuttall Street. Designed by the architect of St Michael and All Angels Church (building 15), it is a Grade I listed building and was built in the Gothic Revival style in the late 1860s. It links with St Columba's Vicarage, also Grade I listed, and forms part of a group with the Sisters' House and Church School, as well as the former Shoreditch Workhouse (now St Leonard's Hospital). Certainly the church's design and warm coloured red-brick exterior, high-pitched gables, tower and slate roofs are a tribute to Brooks' great skill and talent.

The interior of St Columba's is remarkably spacious and lofty and delightfully well-proportioned with solid walls, a wide nave, slender aisles and a central tower. In 1975 having been declared redundant the church merged with St Anne's Church, Hoxton, after which the Christ Apostolic Church (CAC) leased the building and began restoring it. Since then the CAC has worked tirelessly for the

Above and right: Christ Apostolic Church, Kingsland Road (former St Columba's Church).

local community, especially the homeless, and is renowned for its gospel choir. It is presently raising money to pay for much needed repairs to keep the building in good condition.

Station: Hoxton
www.cacbethel.org

21. Shoreditch Town Hall, No. 380 Old Street, EC1

Today a thriving independent arts, live events and community hub, Shoreditch Town Hall's roots lie in its role as a municipal building, within the former borough of Shoreditch. When it first opened the building was regarded as one of London's greatest Vestry Halls (the forerunner of the local council) due to its striking Portland stone exterior embellished with pillars and keystones. The current building is a result of three phases of development, in the mid-1860s, early 1900s and finally in 1937. The tower with its statue of 'Progress' along with the structure to the right appeared in the second stage and this was when many statues and Shoreditch Borough's new coat of arms were added to its façade. The council's motto, 'More light, More power', remains visible all over the town hall, most commonly beneath its crest. It refers to the borough's radical principles and its innovative policies in the late nineteenth century when it was the very first council to construct a generating station burning the borough's rubbish to provide steam electricity for Shoreditch's local industries and people.

The interior of the town hall is quite rare for a building of its type. The ground floor Vestry Hall that was later used as a Council Chamber still features original Ionic columns and sumptuous ceiling roses. In fact, the décor throughout the town hall is grand – demonstrated by its many sculptures, stained glass, red Minton floor tiles

Shoreditch Town Hall, Old Street.

and double staircase. Upstairs, the 1904 Assembly Hall is beautifully lit by skylights and boasts a wonderful proscenium arch displaying masks of comedy and tragedy.

In its early years the Vestry Hall was used for entertainment and was where Music Hall stars such as Dan Leno and Arthur Lloyd performed. In 1888 it hosted the inquest into the death of Mary Jane Kelly, Jack the Ripper's last victim, but ultimately the building went into decline when it ceased to function as an administrative and municipal centre in 1965. It emerged as a major boxing venue for a time, then became neglected before being taken over by the Shoreditch Town Hall Trust, who have been successfully restoring and reviving its fortunes ever since.

Stations: Hoxton, Shoreditch High Street, Old Street
www.shoreditchtownhall.com

Right: Council Chamber, Shoreditch Town Hall. (Ludovic des Cognets)

Below: 'A View of Kneehigh's Ubu!' Entertainment in Shoreditch Town Hall. (Richard Gray)

22. Nos 40–42 Great Eastern Street, EC2

This is one of only few surviving buildings of its kind and a particularly good example of South Shoreditch's great furniture showroom-warehouses, located at the junction of Great Eastern Street and Curtain Road. Nowadays the ground floor is occupied by Stirling Ackroyd estate agents but when the building was erected in 1877 it was designed for the cabinet ironmongers Edward Wells & Co. It later functioned as an auction house, a specialist clothing manufacturer, furniture manufacturers and motor accessories merchant before its mixed-use conversion in the 1990s.

It is not only the triangular position and size of Nos 40–42 Great Eastern Street that has great presence, but it also boasts a wonderful exterior décor with fine blue brick and terracotta ornamentation and magnificent large Gothic arches on its first and second stories. Added to this is the delightful grand Gothic porch

Nos 40–42 Great Eastern Street.

that dominates the building's splayed corner site. The showroom-warehouse was built to the designs of local architect J. W. Brooker, who in his use of Venetian, Italianate and Gothic styles made what would otherwise have been considered a commonplace building into something quite special. Unsurprisingly, Historic England has recognised the significance of the building, awarding it Grade II listed status on account of both its historic and architectural character.

Stations: Old Street, Shoreditch High Street

23. Wells & Co. Commercial Ironworks, Nos 125–130 Shoreditch High Street, E1

This building facing St Leonard's Church (see building 1) is undoubtedly a major landmark of Shoreditch High Street. Constructed in a warm red brick with white stone and mosaics, it displays wonderful Italian Gothic and Moorish features. In fact it is so ornate that it is difficult to believe that the building's original purpose was as a foundry, showroom and shop. Symmetrical in design, Nos 125–130 Shoreditch High Street has two end pavilions, four storeys high and two lower central sections which have high pointed arches on the third storey and enormous wide rounded arches beneath them. The end pavilions continue the pointed arch theme but have flat roofs. Between their third- and fourth-storey windows there is a row of coloured

Wells & Company Commercial Works, Shoreditch High Street.

Decorative features on Wells & Company Commercial Works façade.

inlaid mosaics in the style of the Star of David. Unfortunately, much alteration has taken place since the building was completed in the late 1870s and today, although it is a Grade II listed building, its façade is sadly showing the ravages of time.

Wells & Co. were tenants here for less than twenty years from 1877 but their prominent sign 'Wells & Company Commercial Iron Works' still adorns the building. Edward Wells' business was wholesale ironmongery and he manufactured and sold pipes and guttering, stoves and ranges from his premises. The company also made decorative accessories for the furniture trade that was so endemic in the area. When Wells & Co. moved out in the 1890s the building was initially taken over by a bank, and by the early twentieth century it had changed usage many times and the building was in multiple occupancy. Throughout the 1900s its function changed dramatically; at one time home to a restaurant, a boot and shoe maker, a china and glass merchants, factories and even a cinema.

Today the ground floor is used as retail space – fashionable shops and cafés for Shoreditch's workers and local residents, while the floors above have become luxury loft apartments. An interesting inscription on the central pier of the ground floor between the shops reads 'Contractors to HM Dockyards, Metropolitan Board of Works, Corporation of London School Board'.

Stations: Hoxton, Shoreditch High Street, Old Street

24. The Old Blue Last and The Theatre Playhouse, No. 38 Great Eastern Street, EC2

Renowned for its live gigs and music, The Old Blue Last is one of Shoreditch's greatest night-time attractions. Since the early 2000s when Vice UK took over the building it has both hosted and welcomed numerous bands and singers including the Arctic Monkeys, Kylie Minogue, Amy Winehouse and Florence + the Machine. People have flocked here to see and hear these and many other legendary figures and to soak up the bar's fun and cool atmosphere. The building itself dates to 1876 when it was rebuilt by its new owners, Truman's brewery (see building 9) and gets its unusual name from a cobbler's tool, the last, which is a wooden or metal block used by shoemakers to mould a shoe.

The location of The Old Blue Last is certainly imposing and its circular corner façade striking – as is its conspicuous roofline sign. While the interior of the building harks back to the Victorian era with dark wooden floors, furniture and etched glass, there are no longer any traces of its previous existence in the late 1900s when it operated as an illegal brothel and strip club. Despite its rakish reputation and disreputable past it is today one of the area's most popular venues.

The present building sits on land that was once owned by Holywell Priory, an eleventh-century priory home to Augustinian nuns. When in 1539, under the Dissolution of Monasteries Act, the priory was forced to shut down it was recognised as being one of the country's richest religious houses and its buildings and lands, acquired by the Crown, were demolished, adapted for other uses or sold. In 1576 the actor manager James Burbage leased some of the land and constructed The Theatre playhouse on the site. The building, one of the earliest purpose-built theatres to be constructed in London since Roman times, was polygonal (the first of its type), made of wood and consisted of three tiered galleries and an open yard with a raised stage. In recent years excavations by the Museum of London Archaeology (MOLA) have revealed the remains of the

Below left: The Old Blue Last Pub, Great Eastern Street.

Below right: The Old Blue Last Pub – live music space. (The Old Blue Last)

Bar in The Old Blue Last pub. (The Old Blue Last)

playhouse's foundations close to The Old Blue Last. They are now listed as a scheduled monument.

Station: Shoreditch High Street
www.theoldbluelast.com

25. Nos 134–146 Curtain Road, EC2

It may be hard to imagine today but South Shoreditch was once a buzzing manufacturing enclave where furniture of every type, style, quality and size was manufactured, and the entire district was awash with businesses involved in the furniture trade. It was not uncommon to find small workshops in its tightly packed side streets, often in workers own homes beside furniture factories and warehouses. It could be said that at this time the real assembly line ran through the streets of Shoreditch and for about 100 years (until after the Second World War) this was the country's major furniture manufacturing centre. It was from here that finished goods were transported to specialist stores in London such as Maples and Heals, to towns across the UK, as well as to many worldwide destinations, especially Britain's colonies such as Australia and South Africa.

Curtain House housed the firm C & R Light, named after its owners, Charles and Richard Light. They were qualified cabinetmakers like many of their ancestors had been and joined their father at No. 144 Curtain Road where he had been making furniture since the 1850s. Later, as the firm prospered it expanded into the entire block between Nos 136–144 Curtain Road and became one of the area's most revered and well-known showroom-warehouses. Its product range was simply enormous as can be seen in its 1880 trade catalogue where it advertised almost 2,000 items. Inside the five-storey building the finished goods were displayed on the ground floor and were set in individually furnished rooms so that customers

Nos 134–146 Curtain Road.

could easily locate and view pieces – whether they be for the parlour, drawing room, kitchen, bedroom or even the office or library. The building's upper floors were used for storage of stock and were crammed full of merchandise of every style, ranging from Gothic, Chippendale and Italian to Modern.

When the furniture trade went into decline after the Second World War Curtain House was converted into office space. The building is currently closed undergoing restoration and redevelopment but nonetheless it remains an icon of the area and is a wonderful example of a major Shoreditch furniture showroom-warehouse.

Stations: Old Street, Shoreditch High Street

26. Nos 43–49 Charlotte Road and Gloria Restaurant, EC2

In contrast to Curtain House above, the workshops and warehouses at Nos 43–49 Charlotte Road were a speculative venture and were built for the developer John King Farlow, who in the late 1870s commissioned Henry Hart to erect a terrace of seven four-storey buildings for industrial and commercial use. Walking along Charlotte Road today the buildings appear as two groups yet make up a most impressive block that dominates the narrow road. The buildings are almost a work of art with their pilasters, loading bays and striking white and red brickwork set between the floors and above the windows. They are a marvellous example of how the Victorians embellished their buildings and of their desire to give character to what might otherwise be mundane industrial warehouses.

From the outset the buildings were leased to different businesses. Some but not all were associated with the furniture trade but by the 1980s the entire terrace had been refurbished and all the furniture firms had left. Over the years the buildings saw multiple trades represented here including an umbrella and parasol manufacturer, a lighting company, a manufacturer of coppered steel springs for the upholstery trade, a feather dealer, a furnishing ironmongers and a wholesale looking glass and cabinet makers. Historic England awarded the terrace Grade II listing both for its architectural splendour and for being an excellent example of a typical multi-occupant Victorian warehouse and workshop block in the South Shoreditch area. Today the building is let out as offices, showrooms and for retail purposes.

A few metres down the road at its junction with Great Eastern Street is what has become one of the area's most celebrated Italian restaurants – Gloria. When it opened in 2019 Big Mamma, the restaurant's French dining group owners, took the decision to make Gloria stand out from its competition by reversing the trend that had been prevalent in London for some years of stripping back furnishings to bare floorboards and brick walls to try to emulate the ambiance of Capri in the 1970s. The welcoming greenery beside the entrance door and the bright,

Gloria Restaurant, Great Eastern Street.

Nos 43–49 Charlotte Road.

floral and colourful interior décor, along with the superb Italian food, make this a delightful lunch- and dinner-time spot and Gloria is always busy no matter what day of the week.

Stations: Old Street, Shoreditch High Street
www.bigmammagroup.com

27. The Crown and Shuttle Public House, No. 226 Shoreditch High Street, E1

The Crown and Shuttle has always been a typical East End watering hole since it was built around 1885. The pub was named after a weaver's tool, the shuttle, used by Shoreditch's Huguenot artisans. It was their spindle-shaped shuttles that carried the transverse threads, the weft, through the lengthwise threads, the warp – an important part of the weaving process.

The pub traded for just over a century, becoming part of the Truman's brewery in the 1970s. Within twenty years it had acquired a rather sleazy reputation and became renowned as a strip joint. This culminated in its closure in 2001 and the building was then neglected and left half derelict until it reopened following a major makeover in 2013. The new owners completely reversed the Crown and Shuttle's fortunes by spending time and effort on designing a cool, attractive interior that would draw a young crowd – whether local workers, residents or visitors to Shoreditch. Original brickwork was exposed, wooden mismatched

Left: The Crown and Shuttle public house.

Below: Beer garden, Crown and Shuttle public house.

The Crown and Shuttle public house.

furniture brought in, and a long bar added that extended the length of the pub. The new pub became known, as it is today, for its great range of craft beers and for its super large rear garden (possibly the largest in the district).

Stations: Shoreditch High Street, Liverpool Street
www.crownandshuttle.com

28. Hoxton Market Christian Mission, Coronet Street, N1

Nowadays it is hard to know where Shoreditch ends and Hoxton begins, and in certain respects they have merged as one entity. One thing is certain: both neighbourhoods have much in common and have been challenged by similar circumstances in their past. During the nineteenth century when the districts became increasingly industrialised their populations grew rapidly, with newcomers arriving from every part of Britain and from overseas. Many Irish came here in the early 1800s and found employment as labourers working on the construction of the canals and railways, while Jews escaping the pogroms of Russia and Poland settled here in the latter part of the century. Some of these East European immigrants found work in the local markets while others worked in the ever-growing furniture and textile trades, but many of the immigrants had little work, were horribly poor and housing was in scarce supply.

As there was no national welfare service at this time the unemployed were frequently penniless and unable to feed their families. They were saved from utter destitution by charitable help, often religious missions which would open their doors to provide breakfast or an evening meal and national soup kitchens that served up jugs of soup. In Hoxton one such organisation, the Hoxton Market Christian Mission, became a lifesaver for many of the wretched poor. The mission was founded in 1881 by brothers Lewis 'Daddy' Burtt (1860–1935) and John Burtt (1855–1925), who committed their lives to God's service and undertook to help the underprivileged of Hoxton. From 1886 they occupied premises in Hoxton Market where they ran Christian meetings and Bible classes and locals were encouraged to attend services and sing hymns. Each morning children were provided with food before school and in the evenings the mission would take them and their families to eat free suppers at the Alexandra Trust in the City Road.

Left: The former Hoxton Market Christian Mission.

Below: The former Hoxton Market Christian Mission's foundation stone and brown plaque.

Nowadays the former mission building has been taken over by the MEATliquor bar and restaurant, but the Burtts' great service to the community has not been forgotten and the brothers are commemorated on a Hackney Council brown plaque outside the building's main entrance.

Station: Old Street

29. Village Underground, No. 54 Holywell Lane, Shoreditch, EC2

Launched in 2007, Village Underground is one of Shoreditch's most successful ventures that has brought not only affordable rents to small start-ups and freelance workers in the creative industries but also formed an exciting cultural and creative hub. Furniture designer Auro Foxcroft masterminded the venue and after having persuaded London Underground to sell him four obsolete tube carriages he had them hoisted to sit on top of an old railway viaduct overlooking Great Eastern Street. Two shipping containers he'd acquired were placed alongside the carriages and Foxcroft then went about converting them all for use as studios and office space. He also restored and repaired a warehouse that lay beneath the carriages (the local council made this a condition when granting permission for the development) and transformed it into the most amazing cavernous space that is now used for a multitude of purposes including club nights, live music events, exhibitions, concerts and even theatre and live performance. It is a fantastic music venue and many celebrated DJs including Seth Troxler and Skream have been associated with Village Underground. The warehouse with its high brick walls, vaults and large sloping glass roof lends itself for use for so many events and seems to take on ever-changing identities depending upon its function at any point in time.

Village Underground.

Village Underground encapsulates the very essence of Shoreditch with its cool, hip, colourful tube carriages and containers decked out in vibrant graffiti. As a music destination it is known to be one of East London's best and crowds of young people come to the building regularly and hang out here enjoying themselves well into the early hours.

Apart from its cultural and co-working space roles Village Underground involves itself in social work too, training youngsters, especially from the locale, who want to get a foothold in the music industry. So much goes on within its establishment that it is an ideal place to offer work shadowing experience for those wishing to explore the variety of working opportunities available in the creative industries and to support emerging and struggling artists to achieve their dream.

Station: Shoreditch High Street
www.villageunderground.co.uk

30. Galvin la Chapelle, No. 35 Spital Square, E1

This fine-dining Michelin star establishment unusually occupies the former chapel of a late nineteenth-century girl's school and has one of the most exquisite settings of any restaurant in London today. Since Chris and Jeff Galvin opened the restaurant's doors in 2009 Galvin la Chapelle has won the hearts of its many customers through its remarkable haute cuisine, its discreet but excellent service and the building's magnificent interior. It received its Michelin star in 2011 and

Galvin la Chappelle restaurant.

has never failed to meet the very high standards that such an accolade requires. The two brothers have both worked at some of London's most distinguished restaurants and the dishes they offer demonstrate their vast experience and talent. It is a delight and privilege to sample the beautiful French cuisine and at the same time to be seated in such a stunning building. Before they opened the restaurant the Galvin brothers completely renovated the Grade II listed building (which had been lying derelict for seventeen years) and made a great effort to retain original features such as the granite pillars and wooden ceiling beams. Major highlights of the restaurant are its 'floating' private dining area in the spire section and its abundance of windows that bring in swathes of light to the interior.

Spital Square was first constructed in the 1680s and became the centre of what became known as 'Weavers' Town'. For around 200 years the Huguenot silk weavers, and later Irish weavers too, made this area their home and their workplace. The square, unlike the small alleyways and side roads around it, was built specifically to attract the silk merchants and master weavers and the grand houses certainly reflected their wealth and status. However, as the industry went into decline, buildings were either adapted or lost and the character of the square naturally changed. In

Mezzanine floor of Galvin la Chappelle. (Courtesy of Galvin la Chappelle)

Galvin la Chappelle restaurant. (Courtesy of Galvin la Chappelle)

1890 the Central Foundation School for Girls moved to newly constructed premises here, which included a curate's house and chapel. The latter, now home to Galvin la Chapelle, dominates the somewhat secluded area even though it is only a few moments away from the towering office blocks on nearby Bishopsgate.

Stations: Liverpool Street, Shoreditch High Street
www.galvinrestaurants.com

31. The Old Fire Station, No. 140 Tabernacle Street, EC2

Until 1866 when the Metropolitan Fire Brigade was established there had been no public fire brigades in the country. Previously, when fires had broken out in the capital, they would have been attended to by separate fire insurance companies that had been set up following the Great Fire of London in 1666. Any individual or business taking out fire insurance would acquire a fire marker – a plaque which would be attached to the outside of their premises – and this would act as both a means of identification of the insured and moreover promote the fire insurance company. When blazes occurred insurance company firefighters would rush to extinguish the fires, but it was common for them to ignore buildings on fire which were either uninsured or insured with one of their competitors!

The Old Fire Station, Tabernacle Street.

The Old Fire Station belfry and turrets.

The Old Fire Station opened on the corner of Paul Street and Tabernacle Street in 1896, having moved from its original home in Old Street. It was built at a time of huge construction of fire stations across London and possibly in the period of their most exciting architecture. Shoreditch's station is surely a wonderful illustration of how the Victorians made their civic buildings look grand. The height of the station and use of warm red-brick and stonework immediately attracts the eye, while the building's turrets, belfry, curved stone balconies and cart entranceways combine to make the most pleasing composition. It is a striking building and shows how much effort was put by its planners into its design. As with many stations of this era provision was made on its upper floors to accommodate some of the firemen and their families so that they could be on hand should a fire break out.

Shoreditch Fire Station was operational here until 1964 when a new station was built close by on Old Street. The Tabernacle Street fire station then underwent major conversion and today functions as thirty individual offices with a restaurant facility on the ground floor. With an inner atrium, courtyard terrace and floor to ceiling windows it is a most attractive place to work, and one that still possesses a lot of character.

Stations: Old Street, Shoreditch High Street

32. National Centre for Circus Arts, Coronet Street, N1 (Former Power Station)

In the thirty years that the National Centre for Circus Arts (NCCA) has occupied its premises in Coronet Street it has become one of the most highly regarded circus schools in the UK and today is renowned worldwide. In fact, it is one of only a handful of institutions in the country that runs a BA degree in Circus Arts (in partnership with the University of Kent). Although circus and trapeze acts had been very popular in Britain during the eighteenth and nineteenth centuries, no formal training was on offer for circus skills until the late 1900s. The arrival in the 1980s of the contemporary circuses Cirque du Soleil and Archaos led to a huge revival of interest in this field and today the NCCA provides a wide-ranging programme of courses to those interested in the circus arts. These courses, some lasting as little as a half-day, prepare students, young and old, to learn the skills necessary to become trapeze artists, tightrope walkers, jugglers, stilt walkers and aerial performers. Students can also enrol on recreational termly or year-long courses.

During its lifetime the school has been responsible for training many performers including the aerialists who appeared at the Millennium Dome in 2000 and the disabled Paralympian athletes who performed at the 2012 London Olympics. Included in the school's list of alumni are members of the Royal Shakespeare Company and Cirque du Soleil, actors and theatre directors.

NCCA's attractive red-brick building was built as a power station by the Shoreditch Vestry and opened in 1896. Initially called the Shoreditch Electric Light Station, it later became known as the Shoreditch Borough Destruction and Generating station and its job was to supply electricity to local industries, heat water for the public baths and provide electric lighting in local workers' homes. The electricity was produced here by burning the borough's rubbish (see building 22) and accounts for the Latin inscription that sits on the building's façade – 'E Pulvere Lux et Vis' ('Out of the Dust, Light and Power'). Nowadays

Left: Entrance to the National Centre for Circus Arts.

Below: Generating Chamber – interior space within the National Centre for Circus Arts. (National Centre for Circus Arts)

National Centre for Circus Arts. (National Centre for Circus Arts)

Its interior contains a stunning trapeze and performance studio, an acrobatic studio, a creation studio and rehearsal spaces.

Stations: Old Street, Hoxton
www.nationalcircus.org.uk

33. Former Passmore Edwards Free Library and Courtyard Theatre, Pitfield Street, N1

John Passmore Edwards (1823–1911) was born in Cornwall, in a mining village not far from Truro. One of five children, he was diligent and caring and as a lad helped his father at the family's brewery and market garden. John or 'Jack', as he was known, became an avid reader in his early life and after a brief spell when he worked as an assistant to a local solicitor's clerk, he turned his hand to journalism and moved to London. Here, he was initially employed as a publishing clerk, but within five years had started up several of his own publications, which, despite selling well, failed to make a profit. He became ill and was then declared bankrupt. However, through much hard work he managed to re-establish his career; he paid off his creditors and in 1876 bought the *London Echo*, one of London's main daily newspapers. With his increased status and wealth, he was able to fight for the social and political reform he'd always championed (he had long been a political activist, wanting to abolish capital punishment and the slave trade), and to provide support to the working classes, especially the poor children of London's East End. From 1880 to 1885 Passmore Edwards was the MP for Salisbury but stood down to spend time improving both himself and others. His many philanthropic deeds in London and in Cornwall included contributions to hospitals, museums and galleries, convalescent homes, homes for people with

Above: Entrance to the Courtyard Theatre, former Passmore Edwards Free Library.

Left: Courtyard Theatre. (Guido De Maria)

epilepsy and free libraries. The library in Pitfield Street was constructed in 1899 and in common with all London Passmore Edwards' libraries, received a gift of 1,000 books from him on opening.

When a new library was opened in Hoxton Street in the 1990s the wonderful Victorian red-brick and terracotta library became redundant. It was taken over for a short time by the English National Opera as a rehearsal space before undergoing refurbishment. Nowadays the Courtyard Theatre occupies the lower floors of the building, and it has become a great cultural, music and artistic centre. It is here that many new acts are staged, and young emerging talented artists are given the opportunity to perform.

Station: Old Street
www.thecourtyard.org.uk

34. The Boundary Estate and Arnold Circus, E2

The construction of this unique social housing estate was begun at the end of the 1800s and is said to be one of the first developments of its type built by a local government authority and possibly the world's earliest council estate. The newly formed London County Council (LCC) was responsible for the estate of twenty-three blocks (designed to house 5,524 residents in 1,069 residences), and the estate remains largely council owned today. Unlike subsequent council housing in London the Boundary Estate was planned in such a way that an open central garden space, Arnold Circus, became its focal point with seven wide tree-lined roads radiating off the circus to accommodate the housing. The mansion blocks, four to five storeys high, were largely influenced by

Bandstand, Arnold Circus, Boundary Estate.

the Arts and Craft style of architecture and are still an imposing sight for their height and attractive, warm red-brick exterior. When the estate was built it was deemed revolutionary as it was delivering healthy, dry, open and airy housing to Shoreditch's poor and moreover providing facilities such as a central laundry with bathrooms, a surgery, shops, workshops, clubrooms and two schools.

It was the LCC's intention for the estate to house the 'decent and deserving' poor – a Victorian label describing those in regular salaried employment. The Boundary Estate's first residents were mainly ordinary workers and public servants – nurses, clerks, teachers, policemen – who fulfilled the necessary criteria. This new model housing, however, failed to provide homes to the many poverty-stricken residents of the area who had been displaced when the estate was built. Formerly a notorious slum called Old Nichol, the land had for many years housed the area's most impoverished people, who lived in appalling unsanitary and overcrowded conditions where one in four children died before their first birthday. Sadly, LCC's flagship council housing failed to cater for them, resulting in the poorest moving and creating new slums elsewhere.

Nowadays the estate's buildings are all Grade II listed and lauded for their social and historic significance. Arnold Circus and its eye-catching bandstand is still the heart of the estate and in constant use by the local community and Shoreditch's many visitors.

Station: Shoreditch High Street

Boundary Estate.

35. No. 54 Ivy Street, The Ivy Street Family Centre, N1

No. 54 Ivy Street is surely one of the road's most unexpected, if not incongruous buildings. Part Victorian pub, part play school and part domestic housing, it was the brainchild of the architect Sam Jacob, who co-founded the revolutionary FAT Architecture in the 1990s, a practice renowned for its many unique buildings displaying pop-culture influences. Jacob's building sits alongside a council housing block, ten storeys high and opposite the high brick wall of the Hoxton Garden Primary school built in the latter part of Queen Victoria's reign. At one time the pub, the Queen Adelaide, stood beside a row of terraced housing – the pattern of much of Ivy Street and its neighbourhood up until the Second World War. So many buildings and homes were destroyed by enemy bombing or demolished in the aftermath of the war that the once highly populated streets were left with empty spaces, paving the way for new buildings to replace the old. In 2017 Sam Jacob was looking to build himself a home in Hoxton and saw the potential of a U-shaped plot of land beside the pub. Redundant from the 1960s, the former pub building was then in use as a drop-in centre for the under-5s. Jacob decided to merge it into his new structure and sought permission to extend the buildings above and to the side. He collaborated with the charity running the play group, and agreed to allocate the ground and basement of the building for their centre and built his house to its side. It is unquestionably unusual – bearing a curved prow, tower and a frieze of diamond-shaped windows. If you turn into Ivy Street from Pitfield Street, this is the part of the building that first confronts you, but as you continue towards Hoxton Street the lovely Victorian pub façade catches your eye too!

Below left and below right: No. 54 Ivy Street.

Since its redevelopment the Ivy Street Family Centre has much better facilities and is now able to offer high-quality care supporting the area's young children and their families. Its building has become a real and recognised feature of Hoxton and Sam Jacob's enigmatic house is certainly worth a visit.

Station: Hoxton

36. Imperial Hall, Former Leysian Mission, Nos 104–122 City Road, EC1

One cannot miss this magnificent terracotta building located right beside Old Street and Silicon Roundabout. Dominating both the street and the skyline (it has a striking dome over its central entrance), the building exudes grandeur and could easily have been built as a large department store or even a hotel. Today, Imperial Hall is a residential block of flats and loft space apartments, but it began life with an entirely different purpose.

Designed by Bolton architects J. J. Bradshaw and Gass as headquarters for the Methodist Leysian Mission, it was built to look as non-ecclesiastic as possible so

Imperial Hall, Nos 104–122 City Road.

that it would attract the poor working classes and maybe tempt them away from the evils of drink and bawdy music halls. The mission, founded by the Old Boys of Leys School in Cambridge, opened here in 1903 as a religious and welfare centre, offering legal advice, health services, educational classes and entertainments for the multitude of poor Shoreditch residents. It continued this role for many years but became less necessary once the welfare state was launched after the Second World War. The building was finally sold off in the 1980s and the mission then moved to the Wesleyan Chapel on the other side of City Road.

Station: Old Street

37. The Courthouse Hotel, Shoreditch (Former Magistrates' Court and Police Station), Nos 335–337 Old Street, EC1

Since 2016 this impressive building has been home to the Courthouse Hotel, Shoreditch, part of the international WorldHotels group. Located directly opposite the former Shoreditch Town Hall (see building 22), the present-day hotel is easy to find with its red-brick and Portland stone exterior and royal coat of arms above the grand main entrance and porch. Its architect, John Dixon Butler (1860–1920), dedicated twenty-five years of his life as the surveyor and architect to the Metropolitan Police and in that time was responsible for more than 200 stations and courthouses including Scotland Yard's south building on the Embankment. He chose to design the Shoreditch Court House and Police Station in the flamboyant Edwardian baroque style, which Historic England credits as being 'One of the finest Edwardian civic buildings in London'. Four storeys high, the building was divided into two sections only accessed through the intercommunicating ground-floor cells. The east wing housed the police station, with married quarters for an inspector on its first floor and accommodation on the floors above for forty single

The Courthouse Hotel, Shoreditch.

police officers, with kitchen, mess and storage rooms. The west wing was home to the two court rooms and public access to them was through the principal entrance on Old Street. The interior lobby and double-flight staircase were remarkably opulent, containing a coloured Diespeker mosaic floor, windows by Morris & Co. and a coloured glazed dome. The magnificence of this would surely have overwhelmed many who had to attend court here.

When the Grade II listed building closed in the early 2000s the site attracted movie makers and was where episodes of programmes such as *Spooks* and *Luther* were filmed. It is now one of Shoreditch's most sophisticated and luxurious hotels. It is a cool and stylish five-star destination that boasts its own cinema, luxury indoor swimming pool and spa, a bowling alley, panoramic roof terrace and atmospheric restaurant and bar. Moreover, customers in the Courthouse's bar can sit in an original holding cell where the gangster twins, the Kray brothers, were once detained and imagine how the court would have looked when the celebrated writers George Orwell and Joe Orton appeared in front of magistrates here.

Stations: Old Street, Shoreditch High Street, Hoxton
www.shoreditch.courthouse-hotel.com

Above: Reggie Kray's cell, Courthouse Hotel, Shoreditch.

Left: Bar with cells. (Courthouse Hotel, Shoreditch)

38. Fashion Street Arcade, Nos 10–48 Fashion Street, E1

Turning into Fashion Street from Brick Lane one encounters what appears to be an extraordinary Moorish bazaar. This highly ornate low-slung building extends right along the south (left) side of the narrow street and with its patterned red brickwork, multitude of windows and arcaded ground floor you might believe that you have stepped into an entirely different world from Banglatown just moments away.

The street was first developed with small houses in the late 1600s, which in two centuries had turned into some of the area's most notorious slums. Both the author

Above and right: Fashion Street arcade.

Israel Zangwill (1864–1926) and dramatist Arnold Wesker (1932–2016) wrote about Fashion Street, the latter making it the setting for his highly acclaimed play *Chicken Soup with Barley* (1957).

In 1905 local builder Abraham Davis leased land on the street to build a shopping centre. He hoped to tempt nearby market stall holders to trade here under a covered arcade with 250 small lock-up shops, bathrooms and a reading room. Ultimately only sixty-three shops were built and the project failed, resulting in Davis's eviction from the site in 1909. Since that time the building has had a variety of different occupants but today the premises are home to the British School of Fashion, part of Glasgow Caledonian University.

Stations: Liverpool Street, Aldgate East
www.gcu.ac.uk

39. Zetland House, Nos 5–25 Scrutton Street, EC2

A massive and imposing structure, Zetland House was built at the end of the nineteenth century for Waterlow & Sons as its print works. Extensions were added to the building in the early 1900s and over time the company's premises expanded and stretched across Scrutton Street, Clifton Street and Paul Street.

Zetland House, former Waterlow Print Works.

Waterlow & Sons was founded in 1810 by James Waterlow in the City of London, where he initially produced lithographic copies of legal documents. His four sons joined the family business and continued managing it after their father's death in 1876. The company built up an excellent reputation and in time was commissioned by the Bank of England to print its banknotes. Waterlow's was also responsible for printing the currency of many countries around the globe and thus became a household name. In fact, by the 1920s it was one of the country's greatest printers of banknotes, as well as the printer of postage stamps, bond and stock certificates and letters of credit. Waterlow's work also included all manner of commercial printing and the firm was responsible for travel guides, posters, catalogues, brochures and engraved labels. Following the Portuguese Bank Note Crisis of 1925 the company lost its right to print banknotes but remained trading until 1961when it changed hands and became a subsidiary of Purnell and Sons. After mergers this became The British Printing Corporation (BPC), later part of Robert Maxwell's Communication Corporation (MCC). Waterlow & Sons was finally dissolved as a company in 2009.

When Waterlow's moved from Zetland House in the 1960s about twenty different printing businesses occupied the building and many famous magazines were printed here. However, advances in technology resulted in the building being converted into office space. Sympathetically refurbished, Zetland House has manged to retain many of its original features and occupants now benefit from its high ceilings and large open spaces, as well as an on-site hairdressers, restaurant, café and gym.

Street art on Zetland House walls.

The building undoubtedly has masses of character and in recent times Banksy, the famous street artist and screen printer, was a tenant here. The building's exterior walls are something to see – covered in amazing artwork of Shoreditch's highly talented street artists.

Stations: Old Street, Liverpool Street, Shoreditch High Street

40. No. 55 Pitfield Street, N1

In January 1914 an independent cinema known both as the 'Cinema' or 'Hoxton Cinema' opened at No. 55 Pitfield Street. It was initially highly successful and remained in business for more than forty years (only closing its doors when London was subjected to nightly aerial bombardment during the Second World War). During this period it changed hands once or twice and from 1928 was run by Gaumont British Theatres, who were taken over by the Rank Organisation in the early 1940s. Unfortunately the cinema shut its doors for the last time in 1956, attributing its closure to competition from television, which had become ever more popular with

No. 55 Pitfield Street, Curzon Cinema.

the public. By 1960 Rank had sold off the building and it became home first to a meat packers', then a delicatessen importers and wholesalers and later an artists' studio.

Having become increasingly run-down the building was ultimately demolished in 2016. Architects Waugh Thistleton then designed a new mix-use building for the site (copying the former cinema's façade) containing eighteen residential apartments and a cinema, now run by Curzon Cinema group. It is interesting to note that the former Hoxton cinema had a seating capacity of 866 compared with the three-screen Curzon Cinema's 245 capacity today.

Station: Hoxton
www.curzon.com

41. Gainsborough Studios, Poole Street, N1

From 1924 until 1951 Gainsborough Studios was one of the country's most highly acclaimed film studios and produced a tremendous number of successful movies from its Shoreditch site. Located right beside the Regent's Canal, its premises had previously been the power station of the Great Northern & City Railway and was immediately recognisable due to its large and imposing tall factory chimney. The studios here were originally known as Islington Studios and owned by an offshoot of American film company Famous Players-Lasky, who had had them fitted out with the most modern state-of-the-art technical equipment. Having established the highly successful British Gainsborough Studios, film producer Michael Balcon took over the building in 1924, which he later purchased. It was here that many silent movies, 'B' movies and the later Gainsborough melodramas (targeted at the domestic market) were produced. Due to his charisma and energy Balcon inspired many in the film industry to work at Gainsborough – technicians,

Gainsborough Studios. (Courtesy of IDM Properties)

Hitchcock's head within Gainsborough Studios apartments. (Courtesy of IDM Properties)

directors and performers. In particular, he attracted the greatest actors of the day to appear in his productions such as James Mason, Stewart Granger, Gracie Fields and Margaret Lockwood.

One of the most famous names associated with the studios was Alfred Hitchcock, who began his career working on silent movies in 1921. His first job was as a title card designer writing subtitles for silent films, but he moved into film direction within a couple of years and was then employed by Gainsborough's film director Graham Cutts as an assistant director. In effect, Hitchcock did his apprenticeship at the studios, where he went on to direct some of Britain's best-known films such as *The Lodger: A Story of the London Fog* (1927), starring Ivor Novello, and the thriller *The Lady Vanishes* (1938). Today Hitchcock is remembered at the site by a striking, massive sculpture of his head. The studios have long since moved away and although the red-brick façade on Poole Street remains, the building has been converted by IDM Properties into award-winning apartments which bear the name Gainsborough on the roofline. A local Borough of Hackney commemorative plaque on the building acts as a further reminder of the site's cinematic past.

Stations: Hoxton, Haggerston, Essex Road
www.idmproperties.com

42. The Tea Building, No. 56 Shoreditch High Street, E1

One of Shoreditch's most prominent landmarks, the Tea Building sits at the junction of Shoreditch High Street and Bethnal Green Road opposite Boxpark (see building 46) and Shoreditch High Street Overground station. It opened in the early 1930s as a Lipton's (Allied Foods) bacon curing factory but towards the end of the decade it served as a tea packing and processing plant too – which led to the adoption of its present name. Over the years the building has been used for many purposes. By the 1980s it operated as a department store warehouse and then

The Tea Building.

underwent total renovation in the early 2000s when its current owners Derwent London commissioned architects AHMM to transform the former factory and warehouse into office space.

The Tea Building is eight storeys high and covers a huge area, interconnecting with a neighbouring older warehouse, the Biscuit Building, which was also used as a tea packing warehouse in the twentieth century. Nowadays the Biscuit Building is home to the exclusive private club, Soho House, Shoreditch. The club mainly occupies the fifth and sixth floors and offers deluxe accommodation, as well as three restaurants, a bar, lounges, games room, a spa and fitness centre and fabulous rooftop pool with panoramic views of London. The club is most tastefully furnished and boasts a superb collection of contemporary artworks from artists such as Damien Hirst, Rachel Whiteread and Cornelia Parker, who made their name while living and working in the area in the 1990s. It also contains sculpture and photography of other well-known artists. In keeping with the area Soho House offers a daily programme of events and there is often live music in the evening in the Library Bar.

Every attempt has been made by the present owners to conserve the Tea Building's original features and atmosphere, thus keeping alive the memory

Above: Soho House, Shoreditch, bar and lounge. (Soho House)

Left: Soho House, Shoreditch, roof terrace. (Soho House)

of its industrial heritage. Nowadays the building is a creative hub filled with designers, media companies, start-ups, marketing agencies, artists, fashion brands and retailers such as Pizza East restaurant. In 2007 a new 'street' was added to the ground floor, which allows direct footfall between Bethnal Green Road and Redchurch Street.

Station: Shoreditch High Street

43. The Stag's Head Public House, No. 55 Orsman Road, N1

The present-day Stag's Head is famous for being a major part of Hoxton's and East End London's live music scene and regularly hosts gigs and puts on musical events on its stage. It is a cosy local pub that provides great entertainment while offering attractive food and drink menus.

Built in the mid-1930s, this Grade II listed neo-Georgian pub is an excellent example of an interwar 'reformed' pub, which offered its customers better amenities and greater space than previous pubs had done. Such establishments were more likely to provide restaurant facilities and catered for a wider clientele. This was in complete contrast to the drinking halls of the nineteenth and early twentieth centuries and was largely brought about due to the efforts of the breweries and licensing magistrates to make pubs more family friendly.

The Stag's Head replaced an earlier pub on the site and opened in Orsman Road in 1936. At that time the road was full of industrial buildings including the famous Players cigarette factory, as well as residential housing blocks that made up the New Era Estate. The new pub primarily served the local community and also those working in the area's factories and warehouses – quite different from the former pub's patrons who were largely canal workers.

Situated at the junction of Orsman Road and Halcomb Street, the pub still bears typical features of the 1920s and 1930s Truman brewery house style. Its designer, A. E. Sewell, was the brewery's main architect and the Stag's Head is certainly a fine illustration of his work. The pub is easy to identify from its red-brick exterior, dado tilework and red faience cladding and has a prominent sign with its name and a projecting relief of a stag's head above the main corner entrance. The Truman's black eagle motif can also be seen in an upper niche.

Right: The Stag's Head public house.

Below left: The Stag's Head public house.

Below right: Events space, The Stag's Head public house.

The pub's interior is remarkably unaltered and displays original counters, brick fireplaces, embossed mirrors, panelling and even boasts an off sales area from the period. Customers visiting the pub's saloon bar today continue to be served at the pub's original 1930s Moderne-style curved bar counter.

Station: Haggerston
www.stagsheadhoxton.com

44. New City College, Falkirk Street, N1

The modern college campus on Falkirk Street is one of a collection of further education colleges in East London and Essex that form part of today's New City College. The purpose-built Hoxton campus not only provides excellent facilities but also runs courses that reflect the character of the area, in particular a selection of Creative Arts, Design, Fashion and Media skills programmes. With so many media and tech organisations, galleries and art businesses based in and around Shoreditch, the college offers local young people the opportunity to acquire the necessary qualifications to find employment in the area where they live. The college also specialises in courses related to the hospitality industry. It has its own award-winning training restaurant 'OKN1' where students gain the relevant skills and experience to become chefs and hospitality professionals, and this provides many with jobs in Shoreditch's burgeoning club, bar and restaurant scene.

Entrance to New City College, Falkirk Street.

Above: Interior courtyard of New City College. (New City College)

Right: OKN1 Restaurant, New City College.

Long before the college was built here the site was home to a private lunatic asylum, Hoxton Hall. Having opened in 1695, the asylum was bought by the Miles family in 1715 and was run by them until well into the nineteenth century. Throughout this period the asylum grew to become the largest of many such institutions in Hoxton but received criticism on numerous occasions for its harsh and horrific conditions, overcrowding and maltreatment of its patients. Even so it remained in business until towards the end of the nineteenth century. The institution's buildings were all demolished apart from No. 34 Falkirk Street (today converted into apartments) when it finally closed in 1902.

From the early eighteenth century Hoxton Jewish Cemetery was also located within Hoxton Hall's extensive grounds. Belonging to the old Hambro Synagogue in the City, the burial ground existed here for more than 250 years after which its human remains were reinterred to West Ham Jewish Cemetery. Few records now remain about the cemetery, but it was said to be a peaceful spot containing 500 graves placed among birch and fig trees. A plaque commemorating the former burial ground sits on the wall above one of the main college gates today.

Station: Hoxton
www.ncclondon.ac.uk

45. Boundary Shoreditch, Nos 2–4 Boundary Street, E2

The small hotel sits on the corner of Boundary Street and Redchurch Street (perhaps Shoreditch's coolest and most trendy street filled with independent fashion shops and bars) and is today an icon of the neighbourhood. The building, a former Victorian print works, was bought in the early 2000s by restauranteur and designer Sir Terence Conran (1931–2020), who then collaborated with his partners Peter Prescott and Vicki Conran to design and redevelop the site in a contemporary way. The building didn't simply undergo major conversion but

Boundary Shoreditch. (Elle Pickering)

Above: Boundary Shoreditch roof terrace. (Elle Pickering)

Right: Boundary Shoreditch roof restaurant. (Elle Pickering)

was extended upwards too, giving it two more stories. This created space to accommodate a roof garden and terrace, providing spectacular views of the City and East London. Today it is one of Boundary's most beloved features, ideal for a sundowner or dining with friends in the Orangery and it is in use all year long. The Conrans and Prescott, in establishing their boutique hotel, created seventeen bedrooms that represented an array of individual design themes and furnishings paying homage to famous designers. This has allowed guests to elect to stay in a modernist room in the style of Le Corbusier, another in the style of Sir David Tang or to experience designs of the Eameses and enjoy the comfort of an original Eames chair. In every case the bedrooms contain design pieces of people who have influenced or inspired Conran. All are extremely luxurious, filled with well-chosen furniture and soft furnishings and some contain a separate living room too.

In 2018 Conran sold the hotel to James McCulloch, who founded the Harcourt Inns pub group (famously including the Coach in nearby Clerkenwell and Hero of Maida in Maida Vale). On acquiring Boundary McCulloch decided to upgrade the hotel and give it a new look, so he set about renovating the public spaces to bring them more into line with the current Shoreditch scene. The basement has now become a venue for private events and parties and the upstairs ground floor has been transformed into an all-day brasserie and bar serving a la carte menus, as well as Saturday brunch and traditional Sunday roasts.

Station: Shoreditch High Street
www.boundary.london

46. Boxpark, Nos 2–10 Bethnal Green Road, E1

It is impossible to miss Boxpark – it is like a small village, painted in black with an enormous white sign promoting its name and sits at the major junction between Shoreditch High Street and Bethnal Green Road running beside Shoreditch Overground station. Nowadays it is an established part of and central to the very ethos of the area.

Boxpark is Shoreditch's highly successful 'alternative' retail hub and contrasts with the more conventional shopping centres found at Westfield Stratford City and London's West End. It was the brainchild of the creative entrepreneur Roger Wade, who during the 1990s regularly attended German trade shows where he

Boxpark.

displayed his British Street Fashion brand Boxfresh in a temporary mini shop that was demolished after every event. Realising the futility of this, he went about building a stand in a container that could be used repeatedly, and it was this model that he applied when he launched Boxpark on the former Bishopsgate goods yard in 2011. The first of its type in this country and possibly the world's first pop up mall, Boxpark, Shoreditch, was novel both in its ideology but also in what it offered its customers. Built from more than sixty shipping containers on two floors, it was designed to be both an outlet for authentic street food and a shopping mall selling both familiar and lesser-known independent brands. The company has always supported innovative brands and by offering flexible, short-term and affordable leases it continues to provide space to young businesses and start-ups, small fashion outlets, galleries, lifestyle brands and food stores. Not only a great shopping hub, people come here for events all year round to listen to live music, attend dance classes, DJ and creative workshops, book launches, quiz and comedy nights. Boxpark has established itself as an all-day destination and because of its pop-up culture can accommodate guest brands and invite new independent retailers to promote their merchandise here.

Boxpark beside Shoreditch High Street station.

Boxpark boutiques.

Two further Boxparks have been launched in recent years – in Croydon and Wembley (the largest site to date) – and the company has exciting plans to open a new centre in Liverpool, its first move away from London.

Station: Shoreditch High Street
www.boxpark.co.uk

47. City Road – Contemporary Architecture, EC1

The urban landscape at the eastern end of City Road has been completely transformed in the past decade by the arrival of a cluster of three signature towers belonging to the Eagle and Atlas buildings, and Marriott's Montcalm East Autograph Collection hotel. These enormous glass, stone and aluminium structures with their extraordinary designs are unquestionably an expression of how Shoreditch has changed in the past thirty or so years and represent the area's present-day persona as the face of the country's creative and hi-tech industries. No longer is this a forgotten down-at-heel part of town but it is now 'the' place to live, work, shop and stay on the edge of East London Tech City and Silicon Roundabout at Old Street.

Eagle House, Montcalm East Hotel and the Atlas Building.

The Eagle at No. 161 City Road was completed in 2015 and is a wonderful combination of an original 1930s art deco building along with a striking new twenty-six-storey, elliptical tower. The redevelopment of the site, spearheaded by Farrells architects, shows how well the designers managed to retain the building's context, history and architectural style while adding a contemporary new build alongside it. The old and new seem to blend seamlessly together and the original art deco building is further enhanced by two fabulous eagle statues that flank the rooftop's Eagle House sign.

Right: Montcalm East Autograph Collection hotel room. (Montcalm East Autograph Collection)

Below: Eagle House.

In complete contrast Montcalm East Hotel is a soaring diamond-shaped building that faces directly on to Silicon Roundabout. Its architecture is said to be inspired by the op art of Bridget Riley and at different times of the day the building's grey-silver exterior certainly changes in appearance and colour. The hotel, paying homage to Shoreditch's association with art and artists, has filled its rooms and public spaces with curated art that reflects both the bohemian and creative nature of the neighbourhood.

The third of the three towers, the Atlas building immediately catches the eye with its unique stepped design and graceful vertical lines. Built as luxury residential accommodation, the forty-storey tower has twelve architectural blades that reduce in height and form a slim apex. All three high-rise buildings have added to the dynamism of Shoreditch in the twenty-first century.

Station: Old Street
www.montcalmeast.com

48. Nobu Hotel Shoreditch, Nos 10–50 Willow Street, EC2

This is one of London's, and certainly Shoreditch's, most extraordinary hotels and is located just moments away from Great Eastern Street. Looking a bit like an industrial cruise liner with its concrete overhanging floor slabs, glass and timber façade, the hotel opened here in 2017 and was the Japanese company's first European venture.

Nobu Hotel, Shoreditch.

Its design was due to the combined work of Rod Arad Architects and Ben Adams Architects (the latter taking over the project in 2013), but the interior layout and furnishings owe their design to two local firms, Studio Mica and Studio PCH.

When Nobu Hotels decided to build here their brand was not familiar in Britain, so the company made every effort to build the five-star hotel in a way that would make it stand out from others in the vicinity. The designers were briefed to build a hotel that was not only sophisticated, comfortable and luxurious but embraced the Japanese stye of simplicity while ensuring that the area's industrial heritage was referenced. The results can be seen in Nobu's somewhat raw exterior construction and tasteful internal décor full of colour and local artworks. Nobu's fine restaurant with its courtyard and sushi counter has achieved a reputation for exquisite Japanese cuisine.

Station: Old Street
https://london-shoreditch.nobuhotels.com

49. Principal Place and Principal Tower, Worship Street, EC2

Designed by the internationally celebrated architects, Foster + Partners, Principal Place and Tower sit on the boundary of the City of London's financial district and Shoreditch. Principal Place, facing on to Shoreditch High Street, has been created

Principal Place Plaza.

by the architects as a new public piazza and the residential Principal Tower soars above it on its eastern side as a slender fifty-storey building. The tower is made up of a crucible of three individual sections which differ in height and its apartments have superb views over the City of London and the East End. It is the most luxurious development and has naturally attracted professional bankers, lawyers, creative and technical personnel to move here. The piazza at street level is filled with retail outlets with a range of hip cocktail and wine bars, gastro eateries and a boutique gym. These attract Principal Tower's residents and also local workers such as those working in Amazon's UK headquarters in the adjacent metal- and glass-clad building on the site.

Amazon moved into the innovative building in 2017, which was also designed by Foster + Partners. Working hand in hand with the tech giant, the architects created a widely flexible interior and furnished the building with two spectacular atriums, an acre of rooftop gardens and a fitness studio.

Stations: Shoreditch High Street, Liverpool Street

Below left: Amazon UK headquarters, Principal Place.

Below right: Principal Tower.

50. The Stage, EC2

The book's final entry, a new development, The Stage is exciting for many reasons but perhaps most importantly is its construction above the remains of Curtain Theatre, one of London's earliest known Elizabethan theatres. The Curtain was built around 1577 and is particularly significant as it is one of only a few purpose-built playhouses of the period and confirms that Shoreditch was a cultural hub as long as 450 years ago.

When Museum of London Archaeology (MOLA) undertook a major investigation at the site between 2011 and 2016 it resulted in the discovery of major parts of the original theatre including its internal yard, sections associated with the construction of the stage, two galleries, a gully and corridor. From its excavations MOLA estimated that the Curtain Theatre would have been about 22 metres wide

The Stage residential and commercial development.

Museum of Shakespeare, The Stage. (Cain International)

by around 25 metres long, and unlike other surviving polygonal playhouses of the late sixteenth century in London would have been rectangular or square in shape.

Historic England has now designated the site as a scheduled monument not only for its rarity and survival value but also due to its immense historic interest. We know that the Elizabethan literary giants William Shakespeare and Ben Jonson were greatly associated with the theatre, and it is highly probable that the premiers of Shakespeare's plays *Romeo and Juliet* and *Henry V* and Jonson's *Every Man in His Humour* took place here.

Naturally the developers of The Stage want to highlight the site's magnificent and unique literary connections. So as part of the newly built complex of commercial and residential apartments they have designed a wonderful heritage centre dedicated to the bard's original Shoreditch playhouse. Although at the time of writing the centre has not yet opened, when it does visitors will be able to see the preserved remains of Curtain Theatre, as well as artefacts that were found during the archaeological excavations.

The Stage, like many of Shoreditch's modern developments, is a highly luxurious complex. Designed by the acclaimed American architectural practice Perkins + Will, residents and visitors alike will benefit from its new public square, and its host of boutiques, bars and restaurants, some within beautifully restored Victorian viaducts.

Stations: Shoreditch High Street, Liverpool Street

About the Author

Lucy McMurdo is a modern history graduate and native Londoner who has lived in the capital all her life. In 2003 when she qualified as a London Blue Badge Tourist Guide she combined two of her major loves – history and London – and has been sharing her knowledge of the city with local and foreign visitors ever since. Always keen to explore and learn about London's secrets, she spends many hours 'walking the streets' looking out for hidden corners and unusual curiosities, as well as architecturally significant buildings and ones that have a story to tell.

Lucy's tour guiding career began over forty years ago when she first guided overseas visitors around the UK. Since then, in addition to tour guiding she has been greatly involved in training and examining the next generation of tour guides. She has created, taught and run courses in London's University of Westminster and City University, and also developed guide-training programmes for the warders and site guides at Hampton Court Palace.

Most recently Lucy has been writing about the city she is so passionate about and is the author of ten London books: *Secret Islington and Clerkenwell*, *Southwark and Blackfriars in 50 Buildings*, *The City of London in 50 Buildings*, *Highgate and Hampstead in 50 Buildings*, *Islington and Clerkenwell in 50 Buildings*, *Chiswick in 50 Buildings*, *Bloomsbury in 50 Buildings*, *Explore London's Square Mile*, *Streets of London* and *London in 7 Days*.

Acknowledgements

The author would like to thank all the people and organisations that have facilitated the production of this book. In particular to acknowledge the help and assistance given by Boundary Shoreditch, Cain International, Courthouse Hotel Shoreditch, Courtyard Theatre, Crown and Shuttle pub, Dennis Severs' House, Galvin la Chappelle, Holborn Studios, Hoxton Hall, IDM Properties, Montcalm East Hotel, Museum of the Home, National Centre for Circus Arts, New City College, Saint John's Hoxton, St Monica's RC Church, SAINT Church, Shoreditch Town Hall, Soho House Shoreditch, Stag's Head pub, The Gilbert & George Centre, and The Old Blue Last.

I cannot emphasise enough the enormous role played by my husband, Alex McMurdo, whose many images adorn this book. He has been a continual support whilst the book was being written and has accompanied me on numerous walks along the streets of Shoreditch and Hoxton. Please note that all images displayed without credit are his work and copyright. I am further indebted to him and Jo for taking the time to proofread the text, for their feedback and constructive criticism.

I would like to take this opportunity too to thank Amberley Publishing for commissioning the book, and to acknowledge the excellent support and hard work of Jenny Bennett, Nick Grant, Marcus Pennington and all the team.